In the Grip

of the

Whirlwind

The Armistice Day Storm of 1940

In the Grip
of the
Whirlwind

The Armistice Day Storm of 1940

BY **Tom Powers**

Holt, Michigan

Published by
Thunder Bay Press
Holt, MI 48842

First Printing, January 2009

15   14   13   12   11   10   09   1   2   3   4   5

ISBN: 978-1-933272-20-7

Back cover photo by Harold Holmes from the David K. Petersen Collection. Book and cover design by Julie Taylor.

Printed in the United States of America
by McNaughton & Gunn, Inc.

For Friends and Family

Contents

Wednesday & Thursday

Friday & Beyond

Acknowledgements

Writing isn't quite the lonely business you think it is when you begin listing the organizations and people who so generously lent a hand when asked for help. The Historical Collections of the Great Lakes at Bowling Green University in Bowling Green, Ohio; the Great Lakes Marine Collection at the Milwaukee Public Library; the Great Lakes Shipwreck Museum in Paradise, Michigan; the Michigan Maritime Museum in South Haven, Michigan; and the Meeker County Historical Society in Minnesota contributed invaluable assistance. Carrie Sowden of the Great Lakes Historical Society and Bob Sandeen of the Nicollet County Historical Society in Minnesota went out of their way to help. Dave Petersen at Black Creek Press, Librarian Laura Jacobs at Jim Dan Hall Library at the University of Wisconsin – Superior, and the Winona County Historical Society proved to be invaluable repositories of needed photographs. Wanda Harden at the Flint Public Library in Flint, Michigan provided technical assistance in converting electronic files into hard copy. A huge thank you goes out to Ric Mixter at Airworthy Productions in Saginaw, Michigan for a veritable treasure trove of information he sent the author. Finally, many thanks to Barb who read the manuscript and offered suggestions, served valiantly as the author's computer guru, and listened to the author carp and complain about the writing process. And thank God for libraries and librarians who quietly go about the business of collecting invaluable information and then making it accessible to the general public. Writers would be lost without them.

Author's Note

The Armistice Day Storm of 1940 showcased Mother Nature at her bipolar worst. The late fall weather in the upper Midwest went from near delightful to utterly miserable as suddenly and unexpectedly as a lightening strike out of a clear blue sky. Temperatures fell from the low sixties and upper fifties to below freezing so quickly the Midwest was flash frozen, and within minutes balmy breezes became hurricane-force winds. The impact of the storm, its threat to life, and its toll in damages and suffering lay not only in its ferocity and duration but its unexpectedness.

The huge cyclonic depression's fierce winds, deadly cold temperatures, and freezing rain and blinding snow claimed 154 lives in thirteen states and one Canadian province. Minnesota, at 49 dead, recorded the most fatalities. Among the dead in the Midwest were 26 duck hunters. The moderate weather lured hunters out to their blinds and duck boats in light jackets or even shirt sleeves and then ambushed them with an arctic blast. The Armistice Day Storm has been called the worst hunting disaster in U.S. history.

Hurricane-force winds, huge snowdrifts, and whiteout conditions brought Minnesota to a standstill and wreaked havoc from the Dakotas to Michigan. The storm halted rail, bus, and plane service and closed highways across the Midwest. Towns large and small lost electrical and telephone service. In Minnesota, only its early pioneers had experienced the degree of isolation that descended on much of the state over the next few days.

Winds that often gusted to eighty mph wracked Lake Michigan for more than thirty hours and churned up unusually huge waves. Veteran sailors who lived to tell of the experience called it the worst storm they had ever seen on Lake Michigan. Two Great Lakes freighters and two fishing tugs sank with all hands, a few more narrowly escaped the same fate, and many other ships were driven ashore. The Coast Guard rendered service to forty-eight vessels during or just after the storm, and to some extent, virtually every ship caught on Lake Michigan suffered damage that demanded attention after reaching harbor. The needed repairs meant more time in harbor and less time under steam. The result was a two-million-ton drop in shipping on the Great Lakes for November. The supreme cost was paid by the fifty-nine sailors who lost their lives in the storm.

I don't know where I first ran across mention of the Armistice Day Storm of 1940, but it took several accidental run-ins with the story before the magnitude of the storm fully registered. With my curiosity piqued, I looked for a book-length history of the storm and found opportunity knocking. None had been written.

The two-plus years of research that followed led to incredible stories of great courage, great kindness, narrow escapes, tragedy, faith, strange twists of fate, unexpected humor, and just plain dogged perseverance. The more I read, the more I became enthralled with the hundreds of everyday normal lives thrown into chaos or threatened with extinction by the cyclone. The book leans heavily on contemporary newspaper reports and first-person accounts in the desire to give readers a sense of immediacy as the events of more than a half century ago unfold. Most importantly, I hope this modest narrative does justice to those who lost their lives and those who lived to tell about the great Armistice Day Storm of 1940.

SUNDAY

Chapter 1

"A Climatological Ménage à Trois."

Sunday, November 10, 1940, was the kind of day residents of the upper Midwest expect in September, hope for in October, and pray for in November. Coats and jackets were left hanging in closets as families headed out the door to church, duck hunters shouldered shotguns and cut paths to their blinds, and kids spilled across backyards to revel in the sunny, shirt-sleeve weather. A light breeze stirred leaves, and the low humidity added an extra bow on a summer lover's surprise gift from Mother Nature.

The tankers, ore-carriers, and freighters on the Great Lakes found easy steaming in the mild weather, and few of the sailors at sea or making ready to leave port knew that the next day marked the twenty-seventh anniversary of a storm that had nearly swept the Great Lakes clean of ships in what had become known as the "Big Blow of 1913." Across four of the five Great Lakes, the storm swallowed twelve ships with all hands, littered the rocks, shoals, and beaches of the inland seas with another thirty-one vessels, and took the lives of 253 seamen.

If anything clouded the horizon of sailors and those living in the upper Midwest in the fall of 1940, it wasn't weather but war. German U-boats stalked merchant shipping in the North Atlantic like wolves hunting caribou. France had fallen to the German onslaught with unexpected ease, the Mediterranean ran red with blood, and the Luftwaffe was in the midst of an air campaign aimed at bombing England into submission. The latest war news filled the front pages of every Midwestern newspaper, and the average reader didn't need a crystal ball to foresee the country being drawn inexorably into the conflict. Armistice Day fell on Monday, and for many it meant more than just a three-day weekend. The twenty-second anniversary of the end of the "War to End All Wars" would be memorialized from the Atlantic to the Pacific with parades, marches, and lonely vigils in countless cemeteries. America's looming involvement in yet another bloody European conflict would hang over every parade in the country as surely as a giant, inflatable turkey would tower over the coming Macy's Thanksgiving Day Parade in New York.

But on that warm, sun-drenched Sunday, Midwesterners and sailors alike remained oblivious to a more immediate danger. An immense cyclonic storm was gathering power in the lower Mississippi Valley and inching north. Like a guided missile, the storm and its hurricane-strength winds zeroed in on an enormous bull's-eye overlaid across Lake Michigan, Wisconsin, Minnesota, and their neighboring states.

From the perspective of today's triple-Doppler radar, television weather forecasts promising to predict the differences in weather neighboring towns will experience, and good old tried-and-true 20-20 hindsight, it's hard to understand how the storm could have arrived on the scene so unannounced and unexpected—especially after the storm's opening-day act made such a big splash. On November 7, 1940, high winds roared in off the Pacific and had the Tacoma Narrows Bridge doing a bump and grind a burlesque queen would have been proud to flaunt.

Opened to traffic on July 1, 1940, the bridge carried Washington State Highway 16 over the Tacoma Narrows of Puget Sound. The world's third-longest suspension bridge showed an early and natural talent for swaying and even undulating in the wind. It regularly swayed so much that approaching cars on the 2,800-foot center span would momentarily and disconcertingly be lost from view. The thin, elegant arch of steel and concrete quickly earned the nickname "Galloping Gertie." Engineers came, marveled, and decreed the bridge's sheer mass assured its structural integrity. Well, they should have broken out their slide rules one last time and figured the effect a 45-plus mph wind would have on a bridge that possessed the heart of a pole dancer. On November 7, the public was treated to an engineering striptease as the Tacoma Narrows Bridge undulated, swayed, and began to twist so violently officials closed it to all traffic. One didn't have to be an engineer to know steel and concrete just shouldn't shake like that, and "Gertie" soon began shedding small pieces, then chunks of roadbed broke loose, and finally the entire span fell into the chasm it was designed to cross.

Remnants of the storm swept inland, climbed over the coastal mountain ranges, and spawned a secondary low-pressure pocket on the east side of the Rockies. This depression drifted south and slightly east across Idaho, Wyoming, and Colorado as its barometric pressure continued to fall. When the center of this slow moving cyclonic storm hit the northern Oklahoma border, it hung a sharp left and spent nearly all of Sunday, November 10 tightrope walking the Oklahoma-Kansas border. Throughout the storm's southward slump into the west, weather balloons had charted its course and recorded a wealth of meteorological detail. In and of itself, this low-pressure system was no trifling matter, but when it became the centerpiece of a climatological ménage à trios involving two other weather systems, the tempest that wrecked the Tacoma Narrows Bridge turned into a super storm.

The weather service was also actively tracking an arctic cold front from Canada that had crossed into the U.S. and was moving south through the northern Rockies. The Canadian front played havoc with everything in its path. When the arctic air arrived in Lewiston, Montana, the thermometer plummeted to twenty-one degrees below zero, and Denver watched temperatures drop from fifty-eight to fifteen degrees in 24 hours. The quickly moving front with the super cold temperatures even halted air traffic over the Rockies for a while on Sunday.

Meanwhile, the front that had stormed ashore in Washington continued to edge the Sooner State's northern border where it encountered a warm, moist air mass pushing up into the lower Mississippi Valley from the Gulf of Mexico. The two cold fronts from the north, the one stacked on top of the other, and the warm, moist air from the Gulf began a slow do-si-do to the left. When the fronts met, the hot air rose and cold air fell fueling the storm's already cyclonic winds. As the fronts fed on each other, the storm rapidly intensified late Sunday night and early Monday morning and turned north after lollygagging eastward most of Sunday afternoon. The apex of the storm, where the three fronts met, acted like a figure skater performing a spin. When the skater starts the spin with his or her arms extended, the rotation is slow, but as the arms are drawn into the body, the spin becomes faster and faster until the skater is but a blur. In a weather system, this increasing spin generates enormous power and high winds. The big storm that had come ashore from the Pacific was fast becoming a behemoth that would cover thousands of square miles. The storm's center had eased into a low-pressure trough that pointed straight and true into the heart of the upper Midwest.

The giant storm grew so rapidly and moved so fast it outstripped the era's ability to track it. Conditions in the upper atmosphere provide the best indicators of approaching weather, and in 1940 that meant the use of helium-filled balloons to deliver instruments to the upper atmosphere to measure wind speed, air pressure, and temperature. Airplanes were sometimes used, but they weren't capable of reaching the same high altitudes balloons regularly attained. Balloons took time to deploy and reach those altitudes and were less than reliable in bad weather. The result was that a fast-developing storm with rapidly accelerating conditions could be on the ground before anyone knew it was on the way. The Armistice Day Storm was whipping itself into just such a maelstrom.

By 12:30 A.M. Monday morning, the storm had shaken off the lethargy of Sunday, and the eye was moving northeastward, with increasing strength, through the extreme northeast corner of Kansas. Six hours later, the center of the storm rotated near Iowa Falls, Iowa, and by 12:30 P.M. it was over La Crosse, Wisconsin. The two cold fronts were producing winds in excess of fifty mph and were ripping into the upper Midwest with a vicious one-two punch.

Sunday newspapers in the Midwest reported on the storms and cold fronts pummeling the western states but wrote as if there was no connection to what was happening out west and the weather their readers would soon experience. It didn't help that, as usual on Sunday nights, the Chicago weather bureau office was closed, as were several other regional weather service offices. The November 11, 1940, Chicago Tribune weather forecast told readers to expect a cloudy overcast day with occasional rain and much colder temperatures Monday night into Tuesday morning. The official Indiana weather forecast for Monday also called for a cloudy day with occasional rain or drizzle through Tuesday. One of the worst storms of the twentieth century was rolling into Iowa, Illinois, Wisconsin, Minnesota, Michigan, and up the length of Lake Michigan like a cyclonic gutter ball from hell, and none of the residents in those states or the sailors plying the Great Lakes had a clue it was coming.

MONDAY

Chapter 2

"Steaming Toward Disaster."

The 253-foot *Novadoc*, with a crew of nineteen, cleared South Chicago at 3:00 A.M. Monday morning bound for Port Alfred, Quebec. Built in 1929 in Wallsend-on-Tyne, England, and owned by Paterson Steamship Ltd. of Canada, the *Novadoc* was one of the hundreds of small, nondescript bulk carriers that in its daily, wave-tossed itinerary wove the Great Lakes into a vast, intricate, and colorful commercial tapestry. Generally thought of as a pulpwood carrier, the ship also hauled grain, coal, flour, and coke—not the soft drink, but the stuff derived from coal and used in the smelting process. The freighter was designed to pass through the Welland Canal and deliver cargos down the St. Lawrence and into the Atlantic. Just the past season, the *Novadoc* had almost met a watery end near the mouth of the St. Lawrence, but its cargo of pulpwood acted like a giant life jacket and kept the ship afloat long enough to reach safety.

As the ship passed the Coast Guard Station on its way to open water, Captain Steip, an eighteen-year veteran of sailing the great inland seas, shouted across the water asking for the latest weather report. The request was made because everyone in the pilothouse could see that the barometer was sinking, indicating a low-pressure front was moving into the area. Either Steip's question went unheard or no one manned the station that night because the captain never got a reply as the *Novadoc* headed out into a lake lightly and randomly blanketed in fog.

With the barometer indicating the approach of foul weather, Captain Steip made decisions based on an old and outdated weather forecast predicting a storm with winds blowing from the southeast. He picked the prudent course of sailing the *Novadoc* close inshore up the east coast of Lake Michigan figuring the Michigan mitten's

The Novadoc in better days.

Photo courtesy Lake Superior Maritime Colections, UW – Superior.

landmass would provide a windbreak from the worst of the wind, and if the storm's intensity spiked he would have left himself plenty of sea room to the west.

Old timers will tell anybody who cares to listen that one of the worst places to be caught on Lake Michigan during a bad storm is the stretch of water lying between Ludington and Pentwater, Michigan. The area lies within a large triangular patch of Lake Michigan that has claimed so many ships and seen so many mysterious disappearances it has been compared to the Bermuda Triangle. Little did Steip and many other Great Lake captains, who also thought they had chosen the safe route up or down Lake Michigan that morning, know their ships and the worst the approaching storm had to offer were destined to meet in that very same stretch of water later in the day.

On the northern end of Lake Michigan, two southbound Great Lakes freighters were steering a course that would take them into the history books. Both ships were typical Great Lakes bulk carriers, often called "straight decks" because of the vast stretch of flat deck extending from the back of the pilothouse at the bow to the complex of cabins rising from the stern. The design allowed for enormous cargo holds to be stacked horizontally from fore to aft that facilitated both easy loading and unloading of coal, grain, ore, sand, limestone, and other raw materials. Think of a dozen or even two dozen shoeboxes glued end to end, with a blunt bow on one end and an engine and propeller on the other and you've got a Great Lakes bulk carrier.

Like high-rise apartments edging a seaside cliff, the bulk carrier's pilothouse and Texas Deck are crowded far forward on the bow. In a storm when big waves broke over the bow and slammed into the pilothouse, it was like a boxer leading with his chin. The Texas Deck holds the captain's cabin and quarters for the officers and wheelmen. If the boat has passenger cabins, they would also be found here. The complex of cabins at the stern houses the rest of the crew as well as the galley and dining room. To turn a long walk into a quick trip, crew often ride bicycles across the straight deck when going from one end of the ship to the other. In really rough seas, when the straight deck was often swept by towering waves and momentarily covered by water, the bow and stern may as well have been on the opposite sides of a bridgeless gorge.

The pilothouse, perched on top of the Texas Deck, was lined with windows, and on either side doorways gave access to walkways from which the captain could see the entire side of the ship when entering harbor, docking, or passing through the Soo Locks. There was a starkly Spartan atmosphere to the interior of the pilothouse. A wheel, compass binnacle, and engine room telegraph stood near the center of the room. A chart table might line one wall, radiators offered heat in the cold months, and searchlight and whistle handles were close at hand. In 1940 there were no radar screens, no fax machines that could spit out weather maps or warnings, no weather alert radios, and no GPS devices that could give the ship's location, but ship-to-shore radios were beginning to appear in many pilothouses.

If naval architect J.R. Oldam is correct, Great Lakes bulk carriers are, by design, inherently dangerous. The standard safe ratio of length to depth in a ship is between twelve or fourteen to one.

Since bulk carriers must ply the narrow and shallow ribbon of water connecting Lake Erie to Lake Huron, they have a length to depth ratio of eighteen to one. Other serious design flaws can include weak or faulty hatches and bulk heads that are meant to control cargo but prove all but useless in compartmentalizing water coming in through the hull. Many experts also consider the Great Lake "straight decks" of the era seriously, if not dangerously, under-powered.

These long ships sail on freshwater seas that experienced sailors will tell you are markedly different than the world's oceans. Great Lakes wave action during a storm turns out to be more dangerous than saltwater waves. Fresh-water is significantly less dense than saltwater—as anyone who has swum in an ocean can attest to. Less density means the water, when pushed by the wind, more rapidly builds into waves. Freshwater waves are more steeply-sided and topped with plunging crests that fall on ships like a collapsing building. Waves on the Great Lakes also come in ranks that are more closely packed together. Shallow water, surprisingly, affects wave action much the same as freshwater, so the freshwater and relatively shallow waters of the Great Lakes compliment each other when it comes to producing dangerous waves. This is a major reason why many Great Lakes sailors claim Lake Erie, with an average depth of only sixty-two feet, is the most dangerous of the lakes in a storm. Ocean waves can often run higher than those on the Great Lakes, but waves generated on the inland seas are more numerous and arrive so close together a ship undergoes continuous assault.

In a bad storm, a 400-foot freighter could be turned into two small islands poking up out of a tempest as water covered the deck. One didn't have to look too closely to see the amount of torque waves exerted on 400-foot steel vessel. Big seas hitting the ship from just the right angle could cause the long hull to twist as if the storm was trying to turn the boat into a pretzel. Great Lakes freighters did flex, and a fully loaded bulk carrier could sag as much as five to seven inches amidships. With enough hammering and twisting on the hull, rivets begin to pop and structural failure becomes a possibility.

The *William B. Davock* with a crew of thirty-three had taken on a load of coal Thursday, November 7 at Erie, Pennsylvania and set sail for South Chicago. The 420-foot *Davock*, owned by the Interlake

Steamship Company, had plied the waters of the Great Lakes since 1907. The ship had previously flirted with disaster in a 1909 storm on Lake Erie when she was feared lost only to emerge battered but unbowed from the tempest. The car ferry *Marquette & Bessemer, No. 2,* was plowing the same waters as the *William B. Davock* when the 1909 storm struck. The car ferry went to the bottom with all hands.

After leaving Lake Erie, the *Davock* briefly stopped at Detroit where it took on additional crew, and Captain Charles W. Allen, a Detroiter, took the opportunity to send his niece a check covering her college tuition and post a letter to his mother. The ship had an uneventful voyage up Lake Huron and passed through the Straits of Mackinac and into Lake Michigan at noon Sunday. At 12:15 P.M. Captain Allen broadcast a routine radiotelephone message in which he mentioned the good weather they had encountered on the late season run. Moments later, his ship passed Gray's Reef and turned southwest. Allen's brief communiqué was the last contact with the living aboard the *William B. Davock*, and except for a brief sighting on Monday, the ship would not be seen again for forty-two years.

The regular southbound sailing route on Lake Michigan turned to the southwest after rounding Gray's Reef and took ships between the northwest coast of the mitten and a string of islands that included Beaver Island, the Fox Islands, North Manitou Island, and finally South Manitou Island where ships changed course to pass between South Manitou and Pyramid Point, the northernmost headland of what would become Sleeping Bear Dunes National Lakeshore, and then out into the open waters of Lake Michigan. Once safely past Point Betsie, which lies just north of Frankfort, Michigan, the normal shipping route turned more southward. The picket line of islands stretching from the Straits to Sleeping Bear Dunes offered sailors some shelter from storms coming out of the south and southwest, but once a ship left Point Betsie behind, it faced 200 miles of open water in which storms raged unhindered and undeterred. Ships bound for Chicago, Gary, or any other harbor at the south end of Lake Michigan had to run a 200-mile-long gauntlet of nothing but H_2O that high, sustained winds heaped into walls of moving water that gave new meaning to the term "assault wave."

William B. Davock.

Photo courtesy of the Historical Collections of the Great Lakes, Bowling Green University.

Anna C. Minch.

Photo courtesy of the Historical Collections of the Great Lakes, Bowling Green University.

The 380-foot Canadian freighter *Anna C. Minch* slipped by Mackinaw City and entered Lake Michigan some four hours and sixty miles behind the *William B. Davock*. The *Minch* sat low in the water with 3,134.10 net tons of grain in her holds loaded at Fort William, Ontario in western Lake Superior for delivery in Chicago. The ship departed Fort Williams on November 8 with 260 tons of bunker coal and stopped at Lime Island, in the St. Mary's River, where she took on another 90 tons of coal on November 10. Built in 1903 in Cleveland by the American Shipbuilding Company, the *Anna C. Minch* was the only bulk carrier on the Great Lakes bearing a woman's moniker. The ship was named for a pioneering Cleveland shipping magnate's wife who, after her husband's death, took over ownership of the fleet. The name evidently carried plenty of mojo because no serious thought was given to changing it after the ship was sold to the Western Navigation Co., Ltd. of Canada.

The Canadian ship boasted a seasoned crew, and Captain Kennedy, considered one of the most experienced skippers on the lakes, had commanded the *Minch* for five years. If she was ably manned and led, the old bulk carrier didn't own a clean sailing record. She had run aground twice and been involved in collisions with other ships in 1907, 1916, and 1920. The *Anna C. Minch* was equipped with both a wireless telegraph and a wireless direction finder, but the telegraph was not in working order and regulations then in force did not require that communication devices be carried aboard ships. There was a storm signal station at Mackinaw City, and Kennedy surely cast an eye toward it as his ship passed through the Straits, but the station did not receive instructions to raise the storm warning flag until 6:30 P.M. on Monday evening. By then, all hell had broken loose in the upper Midwest and Lake Michigan.

Following a Canadian tradition, most of *Anna C. Minch's* twenty-four crewmen came from roughly the same local area. In Canada, sailors often got hired on boats through a network of friends, family, neighbors, or just because you came from the same town or area as other crew members. The captain, the first and second mates, and three other sailors came from Collingwood, Ontario. Seven more called the nearby Midland area home, and two others hailed from Owen Sound. The practice made for a tight-knit and effective crew but when, on rare occasions, a ship went down it became a heart-breaking, community-wide tragedy.

Wherever one looked on Lake Michigan that November morning, ore carriers, commercial fishing boats, car and railroad ferries, tankers, general cargo freighters, a wide variety of bulk carriers, and countless other commercial vessels went about their work-a-day life transporting the fruits of North American industry and agriculture from here to there. The vessels were manned by a brotherhood of sailors whose years of experience often made them seem clairvoyant to the landlubber. On moonless, fog-shrouded, storm-tossed seas, they appeared to routinely see in the dark as they piloted freighters through narrow shipping channels or into harbor entrances. Many veteran sailors believed they could sniff out a coming storm with more accuracy that the U.S. Weather Bureau. In ten, twenty, and even thirty years of sailing the Great Lakes, these "old salts" prided themselves on being able to take just about anything Mother Nature and a rogue wave could throw at them. Against sometimes staggering odds, they had sailed their ships through incredible storms and brought them to safe harbor. Spliced into that swagger and freshwater chutzpah was a healthy respect for the lakes and a sure knowledge the freshwater seas could quickly become a boiling cauldron. The Great Lakes required sailors to be ever alert, always careful, and make decisions at the speed of light. Every sailor knew they had to be doubly watchful in November when the worst storms of the sailing season could strike with unimaginable fury and in the blink of an eye, but when you got right down to the cold-hearted truth of the matter, a captain who too often kept his ship in harbor or made for a sheltered anchorage when bad weather threatened was simply scuttling his own reputation.

Chapter 3

"The Maelstrom Hit Chicago Like a German Bombing Run Over England."

At Joliet, Illinois, south of Chicago, the Armistice Day Parade was just about to step off at 11:00 A.M. when the storm galloped into town. Strong, freezing winds followed up by hail that arrived on the scene as if blasted from shotguns scattered both those about to march in the parade and the crowd lining the route. Trees and utility poles snapped in the wind or gouged out huge divots as they toppled over. Blasts of air lifted roofs off buildings with the speed of a bald man loosing a bad hairpiece. Within moments, the storm wrecked the parade and a good part of the town.

Fifteen minutes later, the cyclonic maelstrom hit Chicago like a German bombing run over England. Shrieking winds laden with rain and followed by hail put a halt to the Armistice Day ceremonies and sent spectators running for shelter. Cornices were torn off old buildings and dropped in the Windy City's streets where they detonated like exploding bombs sweeping the pavement with rocky shrapnel. Chimneys blew down, showering streets and yards with flying masonry. Old houses were flattened, and those under construction were reduced to large, messy piles of kindling. The storm felled utility poles and strung live electrical wires across neighborhoods in deadly garlands. Capricious winds tore roofs off some homes and on others first detached and then destroyed porches. On one house, the shingles might have been pealed off with the expertise of an angler scaling a fish while next door windows were blown out and tree limbs sent through the roof. The wall of wind plowed into Lake Michigan with such force it lowered the water level by five feet and, for a time, the Calumet River reversed its flow and poured back into Lake Michigan. The city's lift and swing bridges spanning the Calumet River were closed because authorities feared

16

structural damage. The Chicago Weather Bureau clocked winds at 65 mph while the wind speed meter at the Tribune Tower registered 66 mph—the strongest winds of the century recorded in Chicago.

Along trendy Michigan Avenue, large plate-glass windows, showcasing the merchandise offered in the finest shops to be found in Chicago and the Midwest, burst under the impact of the storm and sent waves of glassy shards scything across sidewalks and into stores.

The ten-story tall Hiram Walker Whiskey sign sitting atop a building at Randolph and Outer Drive, erected at a cost of $150,000, staked a claim as the world's largest electric sign. Seeing as how this was the Windy City, the sign was designed to withstand 100 mph winds. Yet when the storm struck, the much-ballyhooed beacon to booze fell over and landed in the street like a passed out drunk. In other parts of town, the Olivet Baptist Church's three-ton belfry blew down, and a similar fate befell a seven-foot statue of Christ atop Columbus Hospital.

Police reported more than fifty injury cases, most from flying glass, bricks, and falling stonework. Chicago's first fatality occurred when a falling tree struck Mrs. Emily Kerr, 60. The victim was a deaf mute and never heard the splintering crack from the three-foot-thick tree that presaged her death. Paul Hegstrom, 45, sought shelter from the storm against a brick wall which collapsed along with the roof on the hapless carpenter, making him the city's second storm fatality.

Two Northwestern University students made a serious attempt at becoming the city's third and fourth victims while also proving conclusively that academic credentials have nothing whatsoever to do with common sense or basic survival instincts. At the height of the storm, the freshman and sophomore males pushed off from shore in a rowboat that lacked oars or any other means of locomotion except their hands, intent on discovering how far out into the lake the wind continued to blow. A Wilmette coast guard crew rescued the witless pair a half-mile offshore.

Farther a field in downstate Canton, Illinois, a father and two children burned to death when their home collapsed and caught fire. Tragedy struck another Illinois family when a linesman for Peoples Power was killed when the pole he was working on blew down.

In neighboring Gary, Indiana, a railroad worker was blown in front of a train, while the wind picked up a woman in downtown Gary and threw her through a plate glass window. Both survived their injuries. One of Gary's radio stations went off the air when a strong gust felled its 357-foot-tall transmitting tower. The radio station's call letters? W-I-N-D, of course!

Hammond, Indiana ice cream vendor Robert Siemering was not in good humor when the storm imprisoned him in his own refrigerator compartment. Mr. Siemering was working in his ice cream truck's freezer compartment when the storm swept through the city and slammed the freezer door. The vendor had been imprisoned for an hour and was unconscious when rescued.

Chapter 4

"Many on Shore Thought They Had Set Out on a Suicide Mission."

November 11 marked the first day of the commercial fishing season for lake trout and whitefish on the Great Lakes, and two fishing tugs set out that morning from South Haven, Michigan with hopes of cashing in early on the new season. Utilitarian and even austere in design, there is no mistaking a Great Lakes commercial fishing tug as anything but a working boat and a boat that's been worked hard. Even those unfamiliar with the craft instinctively know it is in no way, shape, or form a pleasure boat. These little wooden workhorses might not be pretty or graceful, but what they lack in fine lines, size, or aristocratic bearing they make up for in sturdiness and a reputation for seaworthiness—and they have character written all over them.

The 44-foot *Indian* left South Haven at 7:35 A.M. with an experienced, five-man crew. James Madsen, the 55-year-old captain, had been sailing for years, and Chris Wakid, the second-oldest crew member at 52, had been a Great Lakes fisherman for most of his life. Wakid was not only the *Indian's* engineer but was a part owner in the boat. Bill Bird, Harold Richter, and Art Reeves rounded out the crew. Built in 1914 by the Burger Boat Co., the *Indian* had a succession of owners from the Muskegon and South Haven area. Originally steam powered, the tight little tug had been converted to diesel in 1936.

The *Richard H.* steamed out of South Haven about 9:00 A.M. captained by 28-year-old John McKay Jr., son of the boat's owner. John, married less than a year, drove a laundry truck for his father's laundry when not working on the *Richard H.* Also on board was Stanley White, 33, an experienced commercial fisherman from Rhinelander, Wisconsin, who was making his first trip on the

Fish tug Indian.
Photo courtesy of the Michigan Maritime Museum.

Chris Wakid, engineer and part owner of the Indian.
Photo courtesy of the Michigan Maritime Museum.

fishing tug. John Taylor, 35, was the third crew member. There was supposed to be a fourth, but he hadn't shown up by the time the tug was ready to cast off and was left ashore.

Built in 1923 in Marinette, Wisconsin, the 40-foot-long, steam-powered *Richard H.* was bought by Captain McKay Sr. in 1939. The new owner remodeled the tug which included lowering the superstructure by ten inches. It is not known if any thought was given to replacing the original power plant with a diesel. Some felt the fishing tug was underpowered. A native of

Alpena, Michigan, McKay moved to South Haven in 1936 where he soon owned several boats and a laundry service. This would be the first trip the *Richard H.* made since McKay bought the boat in which he was not on board and at the wheel. Neither boat nor their crews carried any insurance. Likewise, neither South Haven fishing tug was equipped with life rafts nor carried radiotelephones. Their crews had no way of knowing the coast guard ran up storm warnings just minutes after the *Richard H.* left harbor.

No one remarked or remembered seeing the *Indian* after she made her way out past the South Haven breakwater and set course for the fishing grounds around breakfast time. At about 1:30 P.M., the *Richard H.* was sighted five miles out in the lake just as the storm front overtook the boat. Wind ripped the tops off the mounting waves and beat the water droplets into a white froth that cut visibility to zero. The fishing tug disappeared into the white, misty shroud never to be seen again.

In South Haven when the storm struck, there was almost immediate concern for the safety of the *Richard H.* It was generally felt that the *Indian* could take care of itself, but the other boat was smaller and the old steam engine just might not be up to powering the boat through the increasingly huge waves. Concern quickly turned to action. Within the hour, Boatswain's Mate Elmer Dudley was at the dock topping off the South Haven Coast Guard Station's 36-foot surfboat with 200 gallons of fuel. Surfman Kenneth Courtright, Seaman Alvin James, and Surfman Jesse Meeker soon joined Dudley. It was James' day off, but he decided to join the search, "Just for the ride."[1] Equipped with a self-pumping apparatus and a tightly sealed engine compartment, coast guardsmen considered the boat nearly unsinkable. Still, at 2:50 P.M. when the four, foul-weather-clad guardsman cast off the surfboat, many on shore thought they had set out on a suicide mission. In only a matter of moments after leaving port, the boat was lost to view against the driving rain and mountainous seas.

The Pere Marquette Railroad Car Ferry Service proudly boasted, "When the car ferries do not run, nothing runs." The company operated a number of car ferries between Michigan and Wisconsin, and for the next two days the company's ships lived up to the motto. At roughly the same time the coast guard surfboat beat into the maelstrom from South Haven, the car ferry *City of Saginaw 31* departed Ludington and headed into the teeth of the storm. On leaving harbor, the Great Lakes' largest car ferry faced 35 mph winds, but within a couple of hours, endless ranks of two-story-tall waves came barreling out of the southwest and continuously broke over the ship's deck. The really big combers buried the pilothouse which stood 60 feet above the water.

Captain E.S. Cronberg later told reporters, "I've seen worse blows, but they were on Lake Superior. Never a storm like that on Michigan… I spent the entire time in the pilothouse with the helmsman. And most of the time I was hanging on. As it was, I got slapped around from wall to wall all the way over."[2] The crew of fifty-one and nine passengers were also hanging on. Those of the crew not on duty and the few passengers wedged themselves into chairs anchored to cabin walls and hoped they wouldn't also end up "slapped around" by the laboring ferry.

What started out as a little scary and uncomfortable turned potentially deadly early Monday evening when the sea gate at the rear of the ferry threatened to give way under the constant battering. When docked, the gate was raised to permit loading and unloading. On putting to sea, the gate was lowered to keep water from coming over the stern; if it gave way the ship could be imperiled. Crew members rushed to shore up the sea gate with timbers while the ship rolled wildly and waves boarded the ship and sent crewmen ricocheting across the deck.

Burdette Ripley, the ship's cook, reported, "We could look out the kitchen window any time and see wave tops above."[3] The *City of Saginaw's* porter claimed two women spent the entire night clutching chairs secured to walls and over the course of the night, "Didn't say anything."[4] He didn't speculate as to whether they were scared speechless.

Meanwhile, the storm commandeered the ship's whistle and dictated its own eerie cadence that erupted with insane regularity. Spray froze on the whistle lanyard until the cord grew better than three inches thick before it broke off leaving a thick, stubby end that the wind abused enough to make the whistle blow—which it continued to do throughout the night. The storm also destroyed the ferry's radio antenna, cutting off the ship from the rest of the world. Officials in both Milwaukee and Ludington began to worry about the fate of the *City of Saginaw* as the night dragged on and the ferry became six hours overdue. It was with great relief both aboard the ferry and ashore when she pulled into Milwaukee Tuesday morning after what must have seemed an interminable, 13 hour crossing.

In contrast to the *City of Saginaw,* the car ferry *Grand Rapids* carried only one passenger, and Second Officer Clinton D. Martin observed that, "He was too seasick to be scared."[5] Martin said the ship was never in danger even though it faced monstrous waves and screaming winds that often reduced the ferry's forward progress to a one-mile-an-hour crawl. The ship's Muskegon to Milwaukee transit took a whopping 18.5 hours.

Waves swept the deck and even broke over the pilothouse roof. The crew went without eating for 12 hours because they wouldn't risk crossing 12 feet of open deck to reach the dining area. A Grand Rapids sailor with twenty years experience on the lakes and saltwater said it was the worst Great Lakes storm he'd ever lived through.

While the *City of Saginaw* and *Grand Rapids* butted heads with the wind and waves, the storm hounded two other Pere Marquette car ferries as they raced east for the safety of Ludington. *Car Ferry 21,* outbound from Manitowoc, Wisconsin, made Ludington a bare twenty minutes ahead of the *City of Flint,* and its arrival did not augur well for the latter ship. The ferry from Manitowoc entered the narrow channel leading to Ludington Harbor like a NASCAR driver drifting through the fourth turn at Darlington. The captain had one propeller at full ahead and other at full astern, and the ship still couldn't get a good bite against the storm current and high wind. The ship barreled through the harbor entrance, missed Slip #1, drifted past Slip #3, and smacked into the pilings edging the harbor. Smokestack cables twanged then broke, the radio antenna went over the side, and the ship wedged herself tight in the pilings and refused to budge.

Twenty minutes later at about 8:00 P.M., the flagship of the Pere Marquette fleet, the *City of Flint 32,* appeared out of the storm and made for the harbor. It had been a memorable ride across the lake for both crew and passengers. By the midway point of the crossing, the storm and seas were at the height of their fury and did not lessen as the ship approached the Michigan coastline. Normally, the narrow harbor entrance offers no challenge to Great Lakes wheelmen, but in the midst of the worst storm in years, inserting the ferry into the harbor through the narrow channel became the equivalent of threading a needle while riding a Tilt-a-Whirl. Just as it looked as if the crew of forty-five and four passengers were to be delivered from the storm, wind and waves hit the 390-foot car ferry with the perfect combination of blows to send it broadside to the beach and off course.

John Meissner of Ludington, who would later become a Great Lakes captain, was an eighteen-year-old deck hand on the *City of Flint* and on November 11, 1940, could claim a grand total of one month's sailing experience. Naturally, the Armistice Day Storm made a huge impression on the young sailor. As he recalls, "I knew we were in some trouble when we got up to the breakwater and we couldn't bring her around. She wouldn't turn. I was in the fo'c's'le looking out a porthole and I saw the breakwater getting closer. Finally, I said to myself, 'I'd better get the hell out of here.' It looked like we were going to hit something pretty quick. Captain Jens Veevang tried to swing her right to get her inside, but the wind took her left, to the north, so he went north and we slammed up against the north breakwater just inside the lighthouse."[6]

After hitting the breakwater, the *City of Flint 32* was blown north of the harbor entrance and was in imminent danger of being hurled ashore. In a moment of sheer desperation, or genius, or both, Captain Veevang ordered the seacocks opened, and the huge ferry settled onto the sandy lake bed roughly 300 yards offshore with the stern only 60 feet from the breakwater. Fortunately, water didn't find its way into the engine room, and the crew and passengers continued to enjoy heat and light. But just because the *City of Flint* lay on the seabed did not mean she rested easy. Huge waves hammered the ferry and detonated against the ship's side in frothy explosions that sent spume as high as the masthead. The ship rocked back and forth with the waves, and those onboard felt the vessel shudder and reverberate under the constant pounding. The bow had pointed toward shore when she first came to rest on the bottom, but as the night wore on, waves and wind shifted the *City of Flint* until it lay parallel to the shore.

News of the grounding spread quickly through the seaside community, and in spite of the raging storm, carloads of gawkers began turning up on Lakeshore Drive to gaze at the great ship lying stranded and helpless only yards from the beach and just feet from the breakwater. The coast guard, dragging their beach cart loaded with lifesaving gear, arrived on the sand opposite the *City of Flint 32*. Surely, more than a few men from the Ludington Coast Guard Station keeping a vigil over the ship that night wondered if or when they would be called on to mount a rescue attempt in the near impossible conditions.

Chapter 5

"The Boat Turned Everything But Upside Down."

The *Novadoc* and the barometer were heading in opposite directions. As the Canadian ship steamed north up the Michigan coastline Monday morning, Captain Steip watched the barometer continue to go south. The seas had slowly built during the morning, and by the time Lloyd Belcher, a wheelman on the *Novadoc*, gulped down a cup of tea and took over the wheel at noon for his six-hour shift, large combers were racing up from the south and lifting the *Novadoc* as they passed underneath. Within the hour, the captain announced the bottom had fallen out of the barometer clearly indicating the approach of a major storm. Steip considered easing his ship even closer inshore when the wind suddenly swung around and started blowing even harder from the southwest, putting an end to thinking about purposely closing with the Michigan shoreline.

As the afternoon wore on, the size of the waves increased until they were threatening to come aboard over the *Novadoc's* stern. Reviewing his options, Steip concluded it was pointless to even consider making a run for a Michigan port. Trying to pilot the ship through a narrow breakwater or tie up to a pier under the present storm conditions was impossible, yet if he held to his present course, wind and wave could eventually drive his ship ashore. The only remaining option was to bring the *Novadoc* about and ride out the storm with the bow facing the tempest. The captain told the crew he was turning into the storm and warned them of the likelihood of severe rolling.

A long, Great Lakes freighter with its relative narrow beam and shallow draft was always at peril when turning broadside to heavy seas. The threat was ever present that the baguette-shaped vessel would get stuck in a trough between two large waves and roll over. The "Big Blow of 1913" on Lake Huron left several ships hull up in the water looking like giant turtles. Even if the ship didn't turn terrapin, the crew could be thrown around like rag dolls as the ship heeled over then righted itself and rolled the other way.

Belcher hauled the wheel hard to port as the captain asked the engine room for more power, but instead of coming around, the ship hung in a trough and couldn't power its way through the huge seas and into the face of the storm. At the captain's order, Belcher swung the wheel back around, and again the *Novadoc* moved with the wind.

Later, reflecting back on events, Captain Steip couldn't understand why his ship didn't have sufficient power to come about and concluded that either the coal was of poor quality or the *Novadoc* was tossed around so violently that the firemen simply couldn't shovel enough coal into the fireboxes. If the latter was indeed the case, it wasn't from lack of trying on the part of the stokers. Fireman Howard Goldsmith was in his first season on the lakes and he remembered that during the storm, "The boat turned everything but upside down."[7] It was Goldsmith's job to keep steam up to 80 pounds of pressure in the boilers and that meant shoveling coal into the boiler's fireboxes. It was hard work at the best of times but off-the-chart difficult when the ship pitched wildly about. During the storm, the engineers assigned two men to each boiler where they became slaves to 80 pounds of pressure. Each shovelful of coal was an ordeal. First, the stoker had to scoop up a shovelful and keep the coal on his shovel as he braced himself against violent pitching and rolling that threatened to hurl him across the boiler room. The stoker had to hold himself and the shovel load of coal steady waiting until the instant the deck was level before heaving the coal into the narrow firebox door—and then do it again, and again, and again, hour after hour.

At some point in the afternoon while the *Novadoc's* situation was growing desperate but had not yet reached hopeless, Captain Steip spotted the *Anna C. Minch* through the snow, sleet, and blown off wave tops that lashed the pilothouse windows. The *Minch* was making good time and on a heading for Chicago. It was the last vessel the *Novadoc's* crew would see that day. Throughout the afternoon, the size of the waves increased until they were coming over the stern. By 4:00

P.M. Belcher remembers that the now huge following waves not only broke over the stern but momentarily buried the *Novadoc's* decks.

John Peterson had picked the wrong time to help a friend. Peterson was a marine engineer serving temporarily as a stoker for just this one trip on the *Novadoc.* He was standing in for a buddy who needed to be home with a sick wife. From a hospital bed, the experienced sailor would testify before a U.S. Coast Guard board investigation that he and the crew knew by late Monday afternoon their ship was in trouble. Thinking back to that day, Peterson recalled, "We knew that she couldn't weather the gale, but no one said anything for fear of worrying the others. The wind was terrific and the seas mountainous, with driving snow so we couldn't see anything with seas coming over the vessel continuously from end to end. Finally, the seas broke in the door in the cabin in the after end of the vessel where I was."[8]

Belcher's watch ended at 6:00 P.M., but he stayed in the wheelhouse in case he could be of help. Within a half-hour, he was out on deck risking his life helping repair a damaged tarpaulin hatch cover.

Steip decided to attempt turning into the storm a second time and was again unsuccessful, but this time the *Novadoc* wouldn't come back on course and run before the storm. Instead, she wallowed in a cavernous trough and rolled dangerously while the waves took her toward the shore. Eventually, wind, wave, and the wheelman once again pointed the ship on a northward course. John Peterson, that leather-tough old salt serving as a temporary stoker later told the press, "I was born in England and I've spent more than twenty years on the water but that blow Monday was the worst I've ever been through..."[9]

Sure of his ship's fate, the captain sent Belcher below to tell the crew to don life vests and gather in the wheelhouse. The decks were so deeply awash in breaking waves the wheelman couldn't get below, so he headed for the captain's room and hammered on the steel floor to get the crews attention. Belcher then broke out a porthole, stuck his head out into the storm and yelled down his message. Somehow the crew succeeded in making their way to the pilothouse in spite of the fact the indefatigable Belcher found it impossible to get below deck. When the crew from the forward section of ship reached the pilothouse, they instinctively peered out the storm-smeared windows searching the ink-pot black night for the shore they knew was fast approaching.

In a last forlorn attempt to gain some sea room, Steip ordered the engines at half speed astern in hope of backing away from the approaching shore. When that didn't work, he tried again and again to turn his doomed ship into the storm, but the *Novadoc* couldn't force its way through the massive seas rolling in from the southwest.

Someone in the wheelhouse spotted the Little Sable Point Lighthouse from the crest of a towering wave, and as the ship neared the beach, returning waves finally accomplished what Steip hadn't been able to do all day—they turned the *Novadoc* into the storm. Jumping at this last chance to save his ship, the captain called for full speed ahead, and the battered vessel lurched into the huge seas. Within moments, a great wave smothered the bow and smashed into and over the pilothouse blowing in all the front windows. The room filled with flying glass, wreckage, and icy water leaving the crew bloody, bruised, and stunned. The great wave also pushed the bow around, and once again the *Novadoc* was headed toward shore.

Lloyd Belcher was back at the wheel of the *Novadoc* as it was being driven aground and remembers after the captain gave the last order to turn the ship into the wind the stricken vessel wouldn't answer the helm. The storm and the waves had taken control. Captain Donald Steip later reported, "The boat just couldn't compete with the waves."[10] As the ship drifted north along the shore, the crew noted the location of the Little Sable Point Lighthouse from the crest of one massive wave after another. Before the *Novadoc* struck, the engine room flooded when waves caved in the engine room gangway door on the port side. This was a steel door secured with steel bars and clamps; yet, it couldn't withstand the repeated blows from an angry sea. With the fires dowsed, the ship lost power and her lights winked out.

The ship had hardly gone dark when a massive wave lifted the *Novadoc* and slammed it on a sandbar some two miles north of Little Sable Point Lighthouse at approximately 9:30 P.M. When she struck, the crew felt the ship quiver and then break in two. The aft section sagged deeper into the water putting the decks awash.

The pilothouse, minus windows, proved so wet, cold, and utterly miserable, the captain ordered the crewmen in the bow to his cabin one deck below. Belcher and a deckhand braved the fury of the storm to crawl forward and let go the anchors hoping that would prevent the ship from slipping into deeper water. Back in the captain's cabin, the crew lit a coal-oil lamp and took comfort in the light until it ran out of fuel.

Steip, worrying about the welfare of the crew trapped in the aft section of the ship, could find little comfort that night. Minutes before the ship had struck the captain had ordered the men in the stern to the oilers' cabin. Steip hoped that the cabin, located on the lee side of the ship, would offer the men some protection from the pounding waves, but three of the aft section crew never received those orders.

John Peterson had gone off duty and was lying down on a bunk when the *Novadoc* ran aground. The impact threw him on the floor and knocked him out. On coming to, Peterson found himself in a stern cabin with the ship's two cooks when, as he remembers, "… the doors came in on the port side. The cabin started breaking up with water coming through the skylights. We were in danger of drowning, so I tried to get to the starboard side to open the starboard cabin doors to let the water out and dragged the cook with me for he was an older man and couldn't stand the punishment we were undergoing. I managed to reach and open the starboard cabin doors which saved us from drowning. Then the three of us hung on to the port holes. The second cook was in front of the door. I shouted, 'Fred, get away from that door and hang on to the port hole, for God's sake.' Then he started to talk, shout, and swear irrationally. I couldn't understand what he said. Then the water washed him out the door. I couldn't reach him. He hung on to the rail for about ten minutes, then suddenly he was gone. In the meantime, the cook and I were buried under broken parts of the cabin. All I had on was a pair of drawers and a light summer shirt, which enabled me to escape from the debris. Although, I was badly cut by the nails projecting from the woodwork and was barefooted with no boots on which I credited with enabling me to get free. While I was trying to get the cook out, the lifeboat crashed down on him through the cabin, and I couldn't do anything more for him."[11] The bodies of the head cook and his assistant were never recovered.

Alone now, with the cabin coming apart around him, Peterson made for a steel shelter on deck just forward of the after cabins. Hanging on to a safety line someone had earlier strung on deck, he set out for the shelter only to be washed overboard and back again several times. After nearly two hours of struggling in driving sleet, snow, and numbing cold waves that climbed the side of the wreck and broke across the deck, Peterson had worked his way around to a cabin on the starboard side of the ship and forward of the cabin in which he'd watched the two cooks perish. It turned out to be the oilers' cabin, and the ship's engineers spied Peterson through a porthole. As he neared the cabin door, the engineers flung it open and dragged the exhausted man inside where he passed out.

Stranded in the stern section were two engineers, the ship's oilers, and firemen. Captain Steip knew someone was alive back there because he saw matches lit throughout the night. But the question remained: How many and how badly were they hurt? Goldsmith, who was in the aft cabin, remembered shaking from the cold while the seas hitting the low-lying stern, "...shook us to pieces."[12] Tons of water pounded the ship, and in the aft section Lake Michigan came in and at the desperate men from nearly every direction. Peterson was still unconscious when his mates began bailing.

In the ship's forward section, the crew's morale had initially improved after the grounding. They had survived the shipwreck and fully expected to either make their own way to shore or be rescued with the coming of daylight, but the men in the captain's cabin couldn't ignore the unending sledge hammer blows as the seas pounded the hull and superstructure. Some of the crew must have wondered if the wreck could hold together until morning, especially after the door to the captain's room gave out under the ceaseless battering and Lake Michigan poured in. The crew retreated to the captain's office, which was separated from his now awash quarters by a thin wall. If the wall gave way, the seamen would lose their last shelter. It proved a great motivator and inspired the men to spend much of the night trying to reinforce the frail partition with whatever boards and lumber they could find.

The Novadoc, aground.

Photo courtesy of the Lake Superior Maritime Colections, UW – Superior.

A dozen miles south of Pentwater, Michigan, the slim, brick tower of Little Sable Point's lighthouse stands like an exclamation mark over a beautiful stretch of Lake Michigan shoreline. Lighthouse keeper William Krewell had spent the evening atop his 100-foot-tall beacon keeping a wary eye seaward when he caught sight of a ship's masthead lights through the swirling gusts of snow and sleet. The ship remained in sight for almost twenty minutes as wind and wave pushed it north and ever closer to shore. When the vessel's lights winked out, Krewell assumed the ship had run aground. The storm had downed phone lines throughout the state including the line from Pentwater to Ludington, but the light keeper reached the Muskegon light station and informed them of the grounding. Krewell also got through, by phone, to the main Great Lakes Coast Guard Station in Chicago. The latter call resulted in an order to drive to the Ludington Station and inform the officer in charge.

While Krewell headed north, he sent assistant lighthouse keeper Henry Vavrina to the beach in an attempt to signal the ship. Vavrina slogged through driving snow and blowing, eye-stinging sand trying to locate the unknown ship, but he did not see any lights or run across any wreckage and finally returned to the lighthouse.

Chief Boatswain A.E. Kristofferson, commander of the Ludington Coast Guard Station and the officer Krewell had set off to report to, had his hands full. He had dispatched guardsmen to the shore opposite the beached car ferry where they made ready for the impossible task of taking off passengers and crew if it looked like the ship might come apart. Fearing the three-story, steel-clad lighthouse perched at the end of the Ludington Harbor pier was in danger of collapsing under the pounding of mountainous waves, Kristofferson ordered the light evacuated. With the arrival of Krewell, Kristofferson had to find and dispatch men south to the Little Sable Point area.

In every Coast Guard station on Lake Michigan, crews checked equipment and life boats, detailed shore patrols to search for survivors, wreckage and/or bodies, and made ready to transport their breeches buoy and other specialized rescue equipment to storm-battered beaches opposite grounded and wrecked ships. At the Grand Haven, Michigan station, Chief Boatswain's Mate E.J. Clemons was ordered to South Haven where he was to organize a beach patrol extending fifty miles from St. Joseph to Holland, Michigan. The patrols were to look for the oil tanker *Justine C. Allen* that had reported by wireless that her rudder cable had snapped and she was drifting helplessly toward the Michigan coast. The *Allen's* crew saved the ship by jury-rigging a new steering cable, but by then it was feared many other ships in the southern end of lake could be in trouble and the beaches still needed watching. By 4:00 P.M. Clemons had sixteen men patrolling the beach, and they continued to do so in spite of rain, snow, freezing temperatures, blowing sand, and utter exhaustion until Wednesday afternoon. The wind, cold, and the constant drenching from crashing, wind-blown surf left them all suffering from exhaustion.

The U.S. Coast Guard's biggest and best asset for rescuing ships and sailors on Lake Michigan was inexplicably unavailable.

The powerful Coast Guard cutter *Escanaba*, usually stationed at Grand Haven, lay in dry-dock in Wisconsin undergoing annual repairs when the storm struck. Anybody who knew anything about sailing the Great Lakes knew the worst storms of the year arrived in late fall. A question was asked on Monday that would be asked again and again for days and weeks to come. Why would a resource like the *Escanaba* be taken off the board at such a critical time by an organization that should have known better?

Chapter 6

"The Storm Broke the Ship."

By Monday evening, the whole of Lake Michigan writhed in the grip of the maelstrom. Wind velocity held steady on the lake at 75–80 mph with gusts estimated at 100 mph. The lighthouse at Lansing Shoals, nine miles north of Beaver Island, recorded wind gusts at 126 mph. The storm frosted the structure's concrete foundation and grey metal tower in seven inches of ice and blew out nearly all the lighthouse's porthole windows. Enduring the storm in the Lansing Shoals Lighthouse must have gone from exhilarating to frightening and from uncomfortable to sheer miserable.

For those aboard ships that night, to just endure became the central issue. Experienced sailors took no great comfort in being aboard a large ship. Fred Dutton, a veteran Great Lakes mariner whose four-decade career on the inland lakes didn't begin until after the Armistice Day storm, knew from painful experience that huge ships might look invincible but, "…that man's big institutions, which may feel and look solid under your feet, are not. When they go down, they go fast. Ships, banks, and industries."[13]

As with most ships that go down with all hands, unanswered questions and outright mysteries abound concerning the sinking of the *Anna C. Minch* and the *William B. Davock*. From what is known and what can be deduced by informed speculation, it appears that after long struggles the end came fast for both ships.

The *Minch* was seen by the *Novadoc* on Monday afternoon just south of the car ferry route running between Grand Haven and Milwaukee and heading for Chicago. The crew of the *Novadoc* reported the *Minch* did not appear to be in any trouble, but within an hour of the sighting the heart of the great storm swept over the area. The next few hours will always be shrouded in mystery, and no one will ever know for sure how and why the *Anna C. Minch* came to rest on the lake bottom forty miles north from where she was last sighted steaming south.

Wheelmen William Vollick, 35, and Lawrence Thompson, 21, were probably as intimately involved as anyone aboard in trying to keep the *Anna C. Minch* afloat and under control Monday night. Even under the best conditions, steering a Great Lakes freighter is an acquired art. The long ships are contrary beasts that tend to stray off course and go a different direction than the one a captain orders, and every vessel is an entirely different animal when empty instead of fully loaded. The huge bulk carriers also handle differently in shallow water and narrow channels, and many ships are—as the *Minch* was on her final voyage—purposely loaded stern heavy to improve steering.

If it takes a keen hand and great anticipation to man the wheel in good weather, the skill level goes off the chart in bad. A cacophony of sounds assaults the senses and tries to distract the wheelman and the crew. Thunderous bangs and rattles counter-point the banshee scream of wind through the rigging. The wind rips off the tops of the giant seas and hammers walls and portholes with the spray. Mountainous waves climb over the side and crash against the deck and superstructure. Hell, it's a noise that could be fine-tuned for torture.

The wheelman also must continue to anticipate what the ship will do next whether its rolling wildly from rail to rail, shuddering under the impact of waves battering the bow and pilothouse, or being overtaken by waves coming from an aft quarter that slams the already low stern deeper into the water. Just to distract one further, often as not, water sloshes from side to side in the pilothouse and adds wet feet to the quota of discomfort. Steering was made all the more difficult with the pilothouse placed so far forward on the long narrow "straight decks." To help those in the pilothouse get a better perspective when the boat began to turn or drift off course, steering poles were erected that looked like bowsprits on old sailing ships. On the other hand, with the pilot so far forward he didn't have to watch waves board his ship and flood the entire straight deck from the pilothouse in the bow to the crew quarters in the stern.

Whether it was Vollick or Thompson at the wheel Monday night, the storm fully taxed their experience and skill. The ongoing ordeal must certainly have reinforced Vollick's decision to leave the sea. The 35-year-old husband and father of four had told his wife he wanted to quit sailing, and he was back aboard the *Minch* only because he couldn't find a job ashore. On this voyage, William Vollick's fifteen-year-old son Bobby signed on as a deckhand because he wanted to be with his dad.

Lawrence Thompson also had family aboard the *Anna C. Minch*. His eighteen-year-old brother Russell, a deckhand, was in his first season on the lakes and counted on his older brother to help him learn the ropes. The ship contained yet another set of brothers; Howard Contois, 31, a fireman, and his younger brother Clifford, 20, a deckhand.

Since the *Minch* was last seen some forty miles south from where she floundered, old hands assume Captain Kennedy came to the conclusion his ship could not take the head-on battering from the wind and wave and the only hope of survival lay in bringing the *Anna C. Minch* about and running before the storm.

The Canadian Department of Transport's investigation into the tragedy arrived at a different conclusion. Their report pointed out that the *Minch* had a high superstructure in the bow, and this was made more pronounced when she was loaded eight feet by the stern. Loading the ship in this manner improved steering but effectively jacked the bow eight feet farther into the air. Pushing south into Lake Michigan on Armistice Day, the top of the bridge complex rose twenty-eight feet above the waterline while the stern sat very low. In high seas and strong winds, the vast expanse of bow and superstructure could have turned the ship into a floating weather vane. The Canadian inquiry into the sinking theorized that the hurricane strength wind and huge waves roaring out of the southwest pushed the vessel's bow around and the captain had no other option than to turn 180 degrees, fight his way out of a trough—probably with the wind giving the ship a final shove—and run before the storm. In all probability, the above scenario closely followed actual events until the storm delivered a *coup de grâce* that sent the *Minch* to the bottom.

As the day waned, the crew would fight to save themselves and their 37-year-old ship. The veteran captain had to know his ship, like the *Novadoc*, was running out of sea room and huge following seas would have constantly threatened to either drive the freighter to the bottom or wreck it on the beach. Instead, it may have been an inherent peculiarity of fresh water waves—their ability to form large crests that are relatively close together—that doomed the *Minch*. Odds are the end came when, for just a moment, the crest of one great wave raised the bow of the *Minch* at the same instant the stern was propelled upward by another larger comber. Two waves simultaneously raising the bow and stern would have put enormous stress on the middle of the 380-foot hull. The great weight of the fully laden ship which was no longer uniformly supported by water would have broken the *Minch's* back as easily and cleanly as snapping a kitchen match in two. The two sections would have briefly drifted apart before both plunged to the lake bottom.

That Monday night, crewman Gordon Jeffrey's wife lay in a hospital bed in Collingwood, Ontario, holding her new-born baby. Within the space of a few hours, she was both a new mother and a widow. Also lost on the *Minch* that night were Howard Kirton, 35, and his wife, Mabel, 33. The couple, married for seventeen years, had been childhood sweethearts and had sailed together since their marriage. Howard and Mabel were steward and assistant steward on the *Anna C. Minch*. They would be mourned by family, friends, and their dog that in the coming days paced the floor of a friend's house, refused to eat, howled unhappily, and repeatedly searched the street waiting for his masters to return.

The last few hours of the *William B. Davock* can only be pieced together through informed conjecture and a bare minimum of facts. Even though the ship was equipped with a radiotelephone, not a word from the *Davock* made it on the airwaves the day she went down. Since the ship was sighted off Grand Haven on Monday afternoon, miles south of where the *Davock's* life-jacket-clad crewmen began drifting ashore on Tuesday, either, like the *Minch*, the ship was overwhelmed by the storm, driven off course, and forced to run before the tempest, or Captain Allen came to believe coming about was the only way to save his ship. And to confuse the issue even more, the *Petoskey Evening News* reported the *Davock* was sighted approaching Ludington at the height of the storm but unaccountably turned and headed back out to sea during a momentary lull in the whirlwind.

Whatever happened, it doesn't take a psychic to know the *Davock* took a terrible beating. As the ship drove north, countless waves crashed aboard, every one of them searching for a weakness. Jack hammer blows tested doors, portholes, and every inch of the superstructure. Tons of water climbed aboard that threatened to peel away hatch covers or discover another route into the hull where succeeding waves could accumulate and slowly eat away at the ship's buoyancy by the cubic foot. As with the *Minch*, the *Davock's* end came with a heart-stopping suddenness. Whether by wave action or because the captain initiated a turn in an attempt to gain some sea room, the *William B. Davock* appears to have been caught broadside between two towering waves, and before the crew could extricate their ship from the deadly predicament, seas rolled it over and sent it to the bottom. Either just prior to or as the ship plummeted to the seabed, the forward cabin and pilothouse were ripped from the hull.

In the days ahead, many Great Lakes sailors and area locals voiced the opinion that the cause of the double loss was that the *Anna C. Minch* and the *William B. Davock* collided during the storm. Later evidence would make the collision theory unlikely, but doubts remained and the mystery continued to haunt the sinking of the *Davock* for the simple reason that the ship's final resting place wasn't discovered for more than three decades.

Then, there are the UFO theorists and those who believe there are places on the globe where a convergence of unusual forces result in mystery spots within which the unexplainable happens. They argue that Ludington lies near the center of the "Lake Michigan Triangle," a large, irregular pie-shaped wedge of central Lake Michigan where ships and even commercial airliners have disappeared and ghost ships have reportedly been spotted. The triangle supposedly runs from Ludington south to Benton Harbor, from Benton Harbor,

Michigan to Manitowoc, Wisconsin, and then back across the lake to Ludington. UFO devotees believe that the *Davock* was just another in a long list of sailing craft that mysteriously disappeared in the "Lake Michigan Triangle."

If there is one hard, immutable fact known about the sinking of the *William B. Davock*, it was the heart-wrenching grief and lack of closure felt by the families and friends of those who were lost. The families of two-thirds of the crew were even deprived the comfort of having the body of their loved one to bury, and many parents and spouses went to their own graves without knowing, with any exactitude, where or how their sons and husbands perished.

The men serving on the *William B. Davock* came from all around the Great Lakes, but it was Michigan and Ohio that bore the brunt of the losses. Thirteen crewmen came from Ohio and twelve from Michigan, of which eight hailed from the Lower Peninsula's St. Clair and Sanilac counties. Charles Findlay of Ashtabula, Ohio served as a third engineer on the lake carrier *Charles M. Schwab* and through the strange working of fate or the worst of luck found himself aboard the doomed ship on its final voyage. Findlay had been home on sick leave and was eager to get back to work when he heard about an opening as an oiler on the *Davock* for just the one run between Erie, Pennsylvania and Chicago. His wife and two daughters, Joyce, 8, and Jane, 4, waved goodbye as he stepped onto a street car and left for Detroit where he would board the ship. Charles Findlay would never return home. His body was never identified, never found. For the family, his death remained an open wound that never completely healed.

The man Charles Findlay replaced was a twenty-four-year-old oiler named Durwood S. Farr. Love saved Durwood's life and in turn cost Findlay his. Farr was engaged to Marcella James of Ashtabula, Ohio, and the young oiler simply couldn't stand being away from his intended another minute. There were only a couple weeks of sailing left before winter storms and hugely inflated winter maritime insurance rates forced all the "straight decks" off the lakes, and quitting early meant forfeiting a seasonal bonus. That was well-worth the price of love for Durwood, but it made the future Mrs. James none to happy—initially.

Sterling Wood, a nineteen-year-old high school graduate from Lorain, Ohio, was hoping to make enough money to attend college. He had received a $200 scholarship from Baldwin-Wallace College and figured a couple of months sailing the lakes would set him up financially for the next year. Wood boarded the *William B. Davock* on September 21 and counted on his best friend, James Saunders— also a deckhand, to break him in as a Great Lakes sailor.

James D. Bowman, 49, of Lyndhurst, Ohio had served as an ensign in the U.S. Navy during World War I and had been sailing the Great Lakes for two years. His wife Lillian had not seen him since September, and only the day before she had called the shipping line's office to ask if her husband would be home by Thanksgiving. Bowman was survived by two daughters, aged 15 and 13, who had not seen their father since mid July.

Sometime within the next couple of days, Captain Allen's mother would receive a letter from her son dated November 9, 1940. Along with a variety of news, Captain Allen told his mom to take care of herself.

Two other "straight decks" were caught in the same icy cauldron of wind and wave at about the same time and in roughly the same area where the *Anna C. Minch* and *William B. Davock* went down and the *Novadoc* was thrown on the beach like a badly used toy. The 570-foot *Joseph Block* of Inland Steel departed Port Inland 25 miles east of Manistique on the north shore of Lake Michigan on Sunday night down-bound for Indiana Harbor carrying 10,000 tons of limestone. Captain Kizer, like many other captains that day, chose to steam along the east side of the lake because of the prevailing winds and out-of-date forecast.

"At 11:15 A.M. Monday morning," Captain Kizer told the Chicago Tribune, "the bottom suddenly dropped out of the glass. The wind switched suddenly to the southwest, and a gale of 70 mph and heavy seas began to rip at the boat. We headed from a point off Ludington, Michigan, for the Milwaukee shore… If I had headed her directly into the storm, it would have knocked her to pieces."[14] Heavy seas blew out two windows in the pilothouse and caked the wheel and everything else inside with ice. The captain and his first and second mates manned the pilothouse for a 15-hour-long watch.

The *Henry Steinbrenner* had been plagued by accidents, unexpected breakdowns, and just plain bad luck since she was launched at Port Huron, Michigan in 1901. On Armistice Day 1940, the veteran bulk carrier rolled a seven in the cosmic crapshoot while three other ships sailing in the same vicinity (the *Novadoc, Minch* and *Davock*) rolled snake eyes. Burdened with 7,100 tons of coal, the "straight deck" docked at the Interlake Steel company slip in Indiana Harbor after a harrowing ordeal. An endless series of great waves subjected the ship to the equivalent of a front end collision every few seconds. The teeth-rattling jolts sent equipment skidding across cabin decks, and the spray thrown up by the constant battering sheathed the pilothouse and most of the deck in ice. At one point, a colossus of a wave climbed the bow and crashed aboard bursting through the door of the captain's quarters leaving the room awash in broken furniture, clothes, and papers. Fortunately, the *Steinbrenner* was headed into the wind when the storm struck and didn't have to attempt a 180-degree turn and power its way out of a trough. Both Captain Smith and Third Mate Wilbur Cornwell reported spotting the *William B. Davock* during their struggle with the storm. They may well have been the last two people to see the ship before it went to the bottom.

Chapter 7

"Their Uncertain Future."

Until 1957 and the opening of the Mackinac Bridge, the only way for motorists to cross the watery, five-mile-wide gap separating Michigan's upper and lower peninsulas was via a fleet of car ferries that ran continuously between St. Ignace in the U.P. and Mackinaw City at the top of the mitten. When the storm hit the Straits of Mackinac area, it tossed ships around like they were pins in a game of skittles and halted ferry service at 8:30 P.M. Monday night.

The car ferry *City of Cheboygan* rested against the Mackinaw City ferry docks loading cars when the storm reached its zenith. The shrieking wind tore at the ferry with such force the mooring lines parted. With only five cars on board, the recently commissioned ferry—boasting a capacity of 85 autos—left the dock and, regardless of the captain's and crew's wishes, headed out into Lake Huron. The captain quickly regained control of his ship, took her south a few miles, and anchored her between Bois Blanc Island and the mainland with the hope of riding out the storm. By 11:00 P.M. with the ship bucking like a wild horse tied to a post, the crew laid out a second anchor. The five cars on the cargo deck were having the ride of their lives as they were pitched to and fro and inevitably into each other. When the *City of Cheboygan* eventually returned to Mackinaw City, the cars were undriveable and declared a total loss.

Several other ships sought to ride out the storm on the same grounds and anchored near the *City of Cheboygan*, including a laker with new cars lining its deck. In that era, many Great Lakes freighters became car haulers by simply loading new cars on the open deck and tying them down. The storm didn't treat the car hauler any better than the ferry, and throughout the night, new vehicles were seen leaving the freighter's deck faster than bull riders from the back of an ornery Brahmin.

Deer hunting season was only days away when the storm closed the floating highway joining the two peninsulas. The annual migration of rifle-toting Michiganders, in their distinctive red plaid woolen coats and pants, from southern Michigan to Upper Peninsula hunting camps—that most self-respecting homemakers would declare uninhabitable—was near full flow when ferry service came to a halt. Within a few hours, hundreds of cars turned Mackinaw City into a vast parking lot, and before ferry service resumed, deer hunters' cars stretched out of town and four miles south down US-23. Had the hunters gotten themselves and their cars to St. Ignace, they still wouldn't have gotten into the woods because hundreds of downed trees closed most of the roads leading out of town.

Ten ore carriers ducked into St. Ignace during the storm looking for shelter. Meanwhile, a ferry headed for the Lower Peninsula and carrying an unreported number of people and cars anchored midway across the Straits and waited hours for a break in the fury before attempting to dock at Mackinaw City.

Ship captains who decided that regardless of the conditions they would traverse the Straits rather than ride out the storm at anchor found the confining waters an unforgiving place in which to sail during a violent storm. The Canadian freighter *Arthur Orr* ran aground near Waugoshance Point on the west side of the Straits. The 415-foot *Conneaut* had off-loaded her cargo of coal in Milwaukee and was headed back to Lake Erie for another load when the storm caught up with the ship. With a damaged rudder and propeller, the captain decided to anchor at Lansing Shoals and ride out the storm, but the ship broke loose and drifted for eight hours before it ran aground near Epoufette some 35 miles from the Straits. The ride ashore left the ship without a rudder, a seriously damaged hull, and a crew that was most anxious to be delivered to dry land. When the cargoless *Conneaut* rode up on the beach, she was so light she just didn't run aground. With the help of the storm surge and high waves, the ship nearly made it to the beach and was so far out of the water waves didn't break over her.

Tuesday morning, the stranded ship was seen by motorists on rerouted US-2 who reported the unusual sight to the St. Ignace Coast Guard. State police brought a doctor and Coast Guard officials to the wreck by mid afternoon. The tug *Favorite* was dispatched Tuesday and pulled the ship into deep water the next day and towed her to Detroit's Rouge River for repairs totaling $250,000.

From the Straits west to Green Bay, the storm battered the southern shore of the Upper Peninsula but reserved the worst of its fury for the Little Bay De Noc area. The storm surge had the whole length of Lake Michigan in which to build momentum, so when the leading edge of the storm funneled up Little Bay De Noc, it turned the long, narrowing finger of water into a Michigan version of the Bay of Fundy. The wind and roaring crest of water hit with the speed and power of a freight train reducing small boats to splinters, ripping up docks and fishing sheds, and shattering windows. At Gladstone, halfway up the bay, the storm surge lifted fishing tugs from their moorings, carried the craft hundreds of yards inland, and left the boats high and dry as the water receded.

When the storm surge reached Rapid River, at the head of the bay, the water level had risen eight feet above normal. Jim Parent, a fishing guide and owner of a boat rental in Rapid River, was asleep in bed when the surge came ashore and swept his cabin and rental shop back into the bay. Parent was never seen again, but the intact roof of his home/business washed ashore the next day.

Just to prove the old saw about an ill wind blows in somebody's favor, trappers had a field day after the storm. The surge killed countless muskrats that trappers simply picked up like randomly scattered cord wood. Between the muskrats and dead fish tossed on US-2 by the cresting water, it was nearly impossible to drive from Gladstone to Escanaba until all the surf and turf was removed from the roadway.

The storm played havoc with lives and property all over the U.P. In Escanaba, Mrs. Rachel Goss received a rude surprise when she opened her front door Monday night. The hurricane picked her up, tossed her off the porch and against a tree in her yard. She sustained three broken ribs. When the storm roared into Nahma, in Big Bay De Noc, it flattened a dock and threw 700 tons of coal into the bay. Large tracks of U.P. timberland were blown down, the trees all neatly laying in one direction as if they had been felled by a severely anal-retentive, scythe-wielding Paul Bunyon. Fish houses, boats and docks, chimneys, and barns from one end of the peninsula to the other were transformed into debris.

On Monday night, as the storm blew unchecked, nearly fifty ships swung at anchor in Whitefish Bay on the eastern end of Lake Superior, with another twenty-seven anchored in the St. Mary's River, all making a mess of their schedules rather than venturing out into the largest and wildest of the Great Lakes.

Farther south on the morning of November 11, in the then calm waters of Green Bay the 420-foot-long, self-loader *SS Sinaloa* had taken on 5,500 tons of sand from Green Island. Built in 1905, the ship was later refitted with self-loading equipment for handling sand and gravel that literally made it possible for the bulk hauler to suck up the afore mentioned cargo and deposit it in its hold. Great Lakes sailors labeled ships with this unique ability, "sandsuckers."

To head down the bay and reach the open waters of Lake Michigan, the *SS Sinaloa* sailed north, and by the time the ship reached "Death's Door"—the narrow strait which allowed quick passage into and out of Green Bay—the storm was blowing full force. Captain William Fontaine of Buffalo, New York, decided to drop anchor and ride out the storm in this less than confidence building stretch of water lying between the tip of the Door Peninsula and Washington Island. The waters of Green Bay and Lake Michigan meet in this narrow strait where they swirl in dangerous cross currents that have long made widows of Great Lakes sailors, explorers, and Native American canoeists. The place has earned and lived up to its name for more than 300 years.

The hurricane winds bullied the normally turbulent water into heavy and erratic cross seas that pitched the *SS Sinaloa* about like a dog lunging at the end of a chain. When the "sandsucker" began dragging her anchor, Captain Fontaine attempted to move the ship to a more sheltered anchorage only to have the anchor chain part. As the freighter drifted north, the situation went from frayed-around-the-edges to totally unraveled. The radio was knocked out of commission, probably when a wave or high winds ripped away the antenna, and then a steam line ruptured knocking out the steering gear and leaving the ship without power. The forty-one men onboard the *SS Sinaloa* had a long night in which to contemplate their uncertain future as 60-mph-plus winds and huge waves relentlessly pushed their ship north to an unavoidable meeting with Michigan's Upper Peninsula.

⊐☖◁

Michigan's Lower Peninsula hardly fared any better than its counterpart above the Straits. Trees, billboards, chimneys, and the occasional building were blown down, ripped apart, and scattered like chaff. Between Muskegon and Fennville, a village a half dozen miles south of Holland, a traveler tallied sixteen flattened barns. A collapsed barn killed a woman in Spring Lake, and in Grand Rapids the storm leveled a thirty-foot brick chimney, sending it through a factory roof killing one worker and injuring six more. Plate glass windows from Lake Michigan to Lake Erie imploded under the impact of the cyclonic wind. Everywhere one looked, downed utility poles draped power lines across streets, parked cars, lawns, and houses and wiped out telephone service to numerous town and cities. The sagging wires may have looked like limp spaghetti, but they weren't nearly as benign as pasta. Across the state, two people were electrocuted by downed power lines. In Detroit, the storm claimed Michigan's tallest structure when it toppled radio station WJR's 735-foot, $60,000 steel antenna.

Like everywhere in the Midwest, the storm arrived like a stealth bomber. Men in Ludington walked home for lunch in shirt sleeves and returned to work in the same attire. The storm hit from the southwest at 2:30 P.M., moderated some, then struck with renewed fury at 5:00 P.M. By quitting time, 75-mph winds were streaming off the lake. As temperatures dropped, a cold rain froze on the ground and was followed by a blinding snow storm that turned even a short walk home into a life-threatening ordeal. Farmers who happened to be in town that day didn't make it back home for three days. The same scenario was repeated in town after town up and down the state's Lake Michigan coastline.

In a preview of what would shortly and tragically befall duck hunters along the backwaters of the Mississippi River in Wisconsin and Minnesota, the Muskegon Coast Guard Station, by 1:00 P.M. that afternoon, was rescuing duck hunters on Muskegon Lake. Both an oared lifeboat and a powered surfboat were busy plucking hunters and their dogs from remote blinds all over the lake after the unseasonably mild weather abruptly developed into a hurricane that lashed the lake with freezing rain, snow, and waves that small rowboats and the considerably less seaworthy duck boats weren't built to handle.

Rescuing stranded and endangered duck hunters was repeated on the other side of the peninsula when a U.S. Coast Guard lighthouse tender picked up wildfowlers trapped by the storm on mudflats in Maumee Bay near Toledo. Two Canadian duck hunters from La Salle, Ontario, were not so lucky. The storm caught them on Fighting Island in the Detroit River, and although they were less than a half-mile from safety, they froze to death before help arrived Tuesday morning.

The 455-foot-long *George Ingalls* nearly came to grief on the Detroit River at 7:00 P.M. Monday night. The freighter had taken on a load of automobiles at the foot of Iron Street and had just let go its mooring lines and nudged out into the river, bound for Cleveland, when the storm exploded with unexpected fury. Strong winds pushed the *Ingalls* a half-mile north, against the river's strong current, where it came within a hundred yards of smashing into the Belle Isle Bridge before the captain and crew wrestled control of the ship from the storm and got her headed downstream. Farther north, the wind reversed the flow of the St. Clair River and lowered the water level by 2.5 feet. Approximately a dozen northbound ships dropped anchor near the head of the river rather than sail out into storm-tossed Lake Huron. The *Penobscot* did poke its bow into the lake whereupon the captain had second thoughts about braving the storm and returned to the St. Clair River where the ship promptly ran aground.

The greatest peril to Lake Huron shipping occurred when the Port Huron Lightship—in reality, a floating lighthouse marking the entrance to the St. Clair River channel from Lake Huron—was blown 4,000 feet north and 600 feet west of its anchorage. The Coast Guard cutter *Walnut* was dispatched as a replacement until the lightship returned to its assigned anchorage at 7:45 the next morning.

Chapter 8

"The Worst Windstorm
in Milwaukee's History."

In Milwaukee, the storm brought time to a standstill. When the cyclone blew into town, it set the hands of the city hall clock vibrating so severely the clock was stopped and the hands moved to 8:45—a position creating the least wind resistance—until the storm eased late Tuesday. The tempest claimed the same victims as it had in cities and towns throughout the Midwest. Power lines, billboards, chimneys, roofs, trees, and plate glass windows all fell to 54 mph winds that gusted to as high as 80 mph. The debris whipped up by the gusts saturated the air with deadly missiles that wounded hundreds of pedestrians. The whirlwind picked up pedestrians and flung them through windows, against unforgiving walls, and into paths of cars. The icy, wind-driven snow struck unprotected skin almost hard enough to raise a welt. Down trees closed streets throughout the city and the downed power lines plunged many neighborhoods into darkness. The Milwaukee Journal called it, "The worst windstorm in Milwaukee's history."[15]

One Milwaukee man was admitted to the hospital after being hit by a flying door. Another patient spent hours having bits of glass tweezered from her scalp when a plate glass window blew out as she was passing. A ten-year-old girl suffered frostbite to both cheeks while walking home from school. Five hundred emergency phone calls jammed Milwaukee's police and fire departments switchboards as well as the county sheriff's.

Greyhound bus lines cancelled Monday's 11:00 A.M. departures for Minneapolis and Duluth. Semi-trucks and trailers were tipped over by the wind, and passenger trains were delayed for hours.

In the era before affordable, permanent anti-freeze was widely available, motorists prevented their car's cooling system from freezing up by adding an alcohol-based anti-freeze every fall. The trick was judging just the right time to pour the stuff into one's radiator because if the weather turned too warm, the alcohol just boiled away and more had to be added when the temperature dropped. The mercury began a slide that reached 13 above in Milwaukee on Tuesday morning and prompted a city-wide run on anti-freeze by motorists who had been lulled, by the unusually warm fall, into putting off winterizing their cars. Frozen automobile radiators became the car problem of the day across the city and across the Midwest, and anti-freeze quickly disappeared from shelves of most garages and stores.

The storm was no respecter of education. It knocked down the chimney of Milwaukee's Third Ward School and in doing so left a large hole in the roof, but it was not until the wind began shifting what remained of the roof that educators came to the decision to close the school.

Like everywhere in the Midwest, bizarre events continued to follow the storm around like toilet paper stuck to a shoe. The city called on the Coast Guard when a tall smokestack was observed swaying dangerously in the wind. Using skills developed to shoot lines to stranded ships, the guardsmen shot lines over and around the huge masonry tube and maybe for the first time in Coast Guard history tied a smokestack to the ground and kept it from being blown over.

Across town the play *Tobacco Road* was also about to experience an unlikely first. A skylight overlooking the stage imploded just minutes before the curtain was to go up and showered the "Jeeter's Farm" set in glass shards. Since the cast usually performed barefoot, the glass-strewn stage presented a major and dangerous problem, but the show must go on, so for the first time and—one can only hope—last time in the storied history of *Tobacco Road*, the play was performed in house slippers.

It was also not a good day to be an ash collector in Milwaukee on either Monday or Tuesday. Back in the 1940s when many, if not most, homes were heated by coal, ash collectors made regular rounds in the city. Householders would empty the ashes and clinkers from their coal furnaces into containers which the collectors carried out to the street and dumped into an ash wagon. Well, 54 mph winds just played hell with the ash in the containers as they were carried to the street and with the contents of the wagon itself. Within minutes, the wind-whipped ash coated the workers in a ghostly gray from head to foot. The men wore ash, smelled ash, and tasted ash all day, and in every neighborhood in which the collectors worked, the streets and lawns showed a fine patina of off-white grit.

If nobody died in Milwaukee, death did not take a day off in other areas on the east side of Wisconsin that day. Hunters throughout Wisconsin and on the waters of Green Bay were caught unawares by the storm. Two Milwaukee brothers, Roman and Ignatius Zielinski, were in their blind on Big Muskego Lake in Waukesha County just west of "Beer Town" at 6:00 A.M. on Armistice Day morning. Roman, a Milwaukee postman, and his brother had downed three ducks by mid-morning when Ignatius decided to retrieve the birds and set out in their skiff. While picking up the last of the waterfowl, the wind came quick and hard, and it took a supreme effort from the oldest brother to fight his way back to the blind. By the middle of the day, the wind had risen to a constant shriek and the brothers had trouble hearing each other even when yelling in the other's ear.

The Zielinskis spent the night in the skiff covered with a tarp and warmed by a kerosene lantern they had brought under the tarpaulin with them. The lantern ran out of fuel at 6:00 A.M. Tuesday morning. Within an hour of daylight, they ate their last sandwich and decided to try and reach shore. However, the thermometer had plunged to below freezing, and no matter how hard they worked they couldn't outpace the ice that was spreading across the shallow lake and congealing around their boat. Eventually, the ice, too thick to row through but too thin to walk on, stranded them in the middle of the lake. The brothers had been so focused on freeing themselves from the ice they hadn't noticed another boat had drawn quite close to them before it too became frozen in place.

The lone man in the other boat sat quietly hunched over, and every few minutes he would get on his knees, look heavenward, and open his hands upward. Roman and Ignatius weren't sure whether he was praying or begging for the sun to come out. The other hunter didn't say a word to the brothers or even acknowledge their presence when they tried to get his attention. As the brothers watched, the man—later identified as Edward Quick, 47, of Milwaukee—grasped the boat's oars and desperately tried to force his boat through the ice. Realizing the futility of his efforts, Quick crouched on the seat and seemed to withdraw into himself as if to find some reservoir of warmth in his near-frozen body. After a few moments, as the Zielinskis watched helplessly, Edward Quick raised his gloved hands to the sky and then fell forward and came to rest with a lifeless hand hanging over either side of the boat. After Quick's death, the two men covered themselves with the tarp, and while waiting for help they talked endlessly and kicked each other to keep warm. A powerful Coast Guard cutter from Kenosha reached Roman and Ignatius four hours later. Though still conscious, they both suffered from exposure, and each had to be carried ashore on litters. The boat also picked up the body of Edward Quick.

Another hunter in eastern Wisconsin froze to death in his boat only 300 feet from a resort when, once again, his boat had become frozen solid in fast-forming ice. At the chillingly named Butte des Morts, near Lake Winnebago, a sheriff's deputy rescued a hunter who was still alive but encased in ice. Whether by mishap or from the rain, the man's clothes had become sopping wet, and when the temperature fell, his attire turned into an icy suit.

The most unusual means of rescue also occurred near Butte des Morts when Jack West of Milwaukee was out hunting and discovered three hunters in serious trouble late Monday afternoon. The men had somehow managed to strand their skiff in a vast bog. Unable to either walk out of their predicament over the spongy, waterlogged landscape or propel their boat across it, the hunters faced a long, cold, life-threatening night in their boat. West reached the trio by walking across the water-drenched mass of floating vegetation on bog skis. These long, wide, wooden plank-like contrivances are not unlike snow skis, only much larger. At the boat, West found one of the hunters with badly frostbitten hands and feet. West gathered the man in his arms and skied three-quarters of a mile across the bog to safety where he notified authorities. Transportation to the hospital was arranged for the injured man and authorities quickly organized a rescue party that brought in the remaining two hunters.

North of Butte des Morts at the southern end of Green Bay

hunters were treated to the unexpected sight of lake bottom where the bay used to be. The strong winds pushed so much water out of the southern end of the bay the water level dropped by four feet marooning hunters on sand bars and mud banks. One group of seven was caught on a mud bank when the storm hit and repeatedly yelled for help. Eventually, someone waded out to the group's muddy perch with the news they could walk to shore.

Chapter 9

"The Ducks Came and Men Died."[16]

The Mississippi River has always been more than just a mighty body of moving water that bisects the continent. Depending on a person's frame of mind, frame of reference, or where their frame house is located, the river is the Gateway to the West, a great commercial artery, a source of destructive floods, a battleground or a playground, an engineering challenge, a highway, and in the hands of Mark Twain and other writers, an allegory for life itself. In addition to all that, the Mississippi is also a river of birds. It is one of the great migratory flyways in the world, and in any given year millions upon millions of birds follow the big, muddy ditch south in the fall and get their return tickets punched in the spring. This great semi-annual, on-the-wing migration includes five million ducks and fifty thousand geese. The river's broad floodplain with its oxbow lakes and backwater sloughs has long served as the equivalent of an endless chain of Motel 6s and Cracker Barrel restaurants for waterfowl. And, as far as the waterfowl were concerned, what nature created the Army Corp of Engineers improved on. The Corps' ambitious and seemingly endless work of building locks and dams meant to improve river navigation, and the construction of levees, dikes, and vast pools to reduce flood damage resulted in enhanced and expanded waterfowl habitat. Wildlife refuges are strung like jewels along the entire length of the river and, over the years, many projects were undertaken with the sole purpose of improving wetland habitats and providing the public with recreational access to the Mississippi and its bordering wetlands.

All this adds up to heaven on earth for duck hunters. On the night of November 11, 1940, this paradise became a frozen hell on earth, and a fifty-mile stretch of the river—from Prairie du Chien, Wisconsin to Redwing, Minnesota—became a death zone that claimed the lives of twenty duck hunters and an uncounted number of their dogs. Across the Midwest thirty-two duck hunters died.

Every year hundreds of men—armed with shotguns, dragging a veritable train of decoys, bedecked with arcane accoutrements only a fellow waterfowler could identify, and followed by their retrievers— invade the Mississippi wetlands of the upper Midwest and invariably pray for bad weather. Duck hunters revel in cold, rainy, windy conditions with some snow flurries thrown in for good measure. If it's the kind of weather any apparently sane person would only enjoy while at home in front of a cozy fire, it's the very conditions hunters welcome in a roofless duck blind or when laying with their face to the sky in a cramped duck boat. One of the first rules a hunter learns about migrating ducks and geese is that waterfowl generally only move in good numbers in bad weather. The weather was so good— by non hunting standards—on Armistice Day morning and on the days leading up to it some duck hunters stayed home.

Unfortunately, if the hundreds of hunters who shouldered their Brownings, Ithacas, and Remingtons and moved into blinds and firing positions along the upper Mississippi that morning hoped or prayed for bad weather, they didn't dress for it. On an unusually mild November morning hinting at fifty-degree temperatures by afternoon, many men left home as if dressed for September 11 rather than November 11. Few thought to pack survival gear, gloves, and their old woolen hat or even rain gear. If the weather changed suddenly and violently, home and a new set of clothes or the forgotten wool hunting coat and the insulated, waterproof boots were not a block away. Help of any sort was not even a dozen blocks away.

The Mississippi riverine landscape is surprisingly vast. The river itself can be more than a mile across, and its floodplain of diked pools, open marshes, and swampy woodland often reaches several miles in width before encountering the rising ground that builds into the palisade of bluffs that line the Mississippi. The pools and backwater sloughs often rival large inland lakes in size and sport a variety of habitat ranging from deep quiet water to shallow marshland interrupted by dikes, woody islands, and sand spits that barely manage to rise above the surrounding water. If the weather

Hunters in shirt-sleeves setting up a blind overlooking
Mississippi wetlands near Winona just days before the storm.
Photo courtesy of the Winona County Historical Society.

turns bad enough to obscure distant landmarks or the sun goes down
on a moonless night, it's easy to become disoriented and lost.

As any experienced duck hunter could have predicted, hunting
wasn't very good early Monday morning. Regardless of the warm
weather, hundreds planned to spend Armistice Day on the Mississippi
backwaters hunting, and both prospects and moods rose when
conditions began to deteriorate around mid-morning. Temperatures
dipped, the wind kicked up, rain fell, and waterfowl began to move
in small groups then in the hundreds. When the wind hit gale force
and the rain turned to sleet, snow hunters thought they had found
nirvana. Ducks were moving in the thousands. Many hunters got
their limit and could have, in the first hour or two of the storm,
filled the bed of a pickup with birds.

Donald Henkel of Duluth was out duck hunting with his
dad, grandfather, and uncle in two-man duck boats on November
11. His most vivid memory of the day was the sight of hundreds
of thousands of waterfowl blackening the sky as they fled before
the approaching storm. The young man was awestruck by the great
flights of waterfowl packed wingtip to wingtip that stretched from

horizon to horizon. Men forgot about their own safety in this once-in-a-lifetime hunting opportunity as the great masses of birds took wing and—with better instincts than most hunters—sought shelter from the storm.

Ducks came hurtling past blinds and shooting stations from every direction. With the wind at their backs, ducks rocketed past blinds like F-15s with afterburners lit. On the rare occasion when a bird headed into the wind, hunters saw ducks' forward progress reduced to slow motion. Targets were everywhere, but they were becoming hard to hit as the gale played havoc with birdshot. When shooting across the wind, the shot trajectory bent like a curveball and firing directly into the wind muffled it like a pillow.

Most hunters realized too late that the weather had gone from gloriously miserable to life threatening. In La Crosse, Wisconsin, thermometers read 52 degrees at 4:30 A.M., 25 degrees at 9:35 A.M., and by 3:25 P.M. registered a bone-chilling 14 degrees above zero. The winds hit the impoundments, backwater sloughs, and the Mississippi itself like a wave machine from hell and almost instantly churned up five and six foot rolling breakers against which small skiffs, canoes, and low freeboard duck boats didn't stand a chance. Even in the smaller pools and sloughs where the wind didn't have the reach to create big waves, it was still impossible for a man to make any headway if rowing into the teeth of the wailing banshee. In the rain and sleet, dry clothes became essential for survival, especially if the hunter had left his wool clothes at home, because wet cotton isn't worth a diddley-damn as insulation.

At some point in the afternoon, it was as if the hunters became the prey and not the ducks. Harrowing life and death struggles became commonplace in the Mississippi bottomlands from Illinois to Minnesota. Many hunters in light clothing realized the gravity of their situation and knew they couldn't survive the coming night outside and pushed themselves toward home or shelter. Some panicked and died while others, like Mr. Jueneman, a well-known barber from the small town of Wabasha, Minnesota, succumbed from bad luck. The barber had all the right clothing and equipment, but when his boat overturned in the storm, Jueneman's wool coat, heavy clothing, and hunting boots dragged him under. His hunting partner somehow managed to swim to shore—he must have been lightly clothed—and hurriedly organized a search party, but the high waves made it impossible to launch a boat. The barber left a wife and two children.

Dan Kukowski of Winona, Minnesota, somehow lucked out. Although he lived in Minnesota, Dan hunted from an island near the Wisconsin shore, so he rode his bike over the Mississippi to where he beached his canoe and paddled out to his blind. Dan remembers cold rain and wind set in about 11:00 A.M., and the storm front pushed thousands of ducks in front of it. It soon got so windy that when a hunter nailed a duck the wind often blew it beyond reach. Kukowski saw one hunter pull his dog under his raincoat and hug him for dear life. The dog's body heat probably saved his life. Dan also recalls seeing another friend sitting against a tree frozen to death. By 4:30 in the afternoon, Dan felt that his best chance for survival came down to paddling all the way across the river to Minnesota—which in retrospect seems suicidal. The waves had grown so tall Kukowski couldn't see over them from his canoe seat, and the wind sheered off the top of the watery crests and drove the spindrift at the desperate canoeist like he was at the receiving end of a power washer. Kukowski thought his time was up but kept paddling. At home, worry had reduced his wife to tears. A friend on the Minnesota side watched as he fought his way across the river and met him when he miraculously beached his twelve-foot canoe on the Minnesota shore.

Throughout Monday afternoon and night, little miracles or the absence thereof meant the difference between life and death on the Mississippi floodplain. The Strasser brothers of St. Paul, Minnesota, had downed a good number of ducks from an island in the river near Wabasha when the weather went from good duck hunting to truly nasty. Sensing danger, the brothers pulled in their decoys only to discover they may have waited too long. The open water lying between the island and the Minnesota shore had built into endless ranks of three-foot waves marching across the water. Both brothers figured their chances were slim on reaching the Minnesota shore in their little oar-powered duck boat but better than staying on the island and surely freezing to death. They emptied the boat of everything but their guns and set off with the idea of rowing with the waves and slowly working the boat across to the far shore without ever getting broadside to the waves.

The brothers' cold, miserable, frightening voyage had all but beaten the odds and they were within a hundred feet of shore when the river wrenched the oars out of the oarlocks and washed them away, then spun the small boat broadside to the waves. In the time it takes to release the safety and pull the triggers of a double-barreled shotgun, the boat sunk beneath them and left the brothers facing almost certain death. Then, out of nowhere, a huge wave lifted the two men and threw them shoreward and into water shallow enough they could wade to dry land. A second, maybe smaller, miracle occurred when the two sopping-wet men staggered ashore close enough to a farmhouse they could reach before their clothes and bodies froze rock hard.

Those who couldn't make it off the water tried everything to keep warm. Decoys were burned and boats were turned over to provide shelter, and in some cases they, too, were burned. Hunters stranded near stands of timber started fires with downed wood then used their shotguns to blast dead branches from the trees. Men tried to keep warm by performing jumping jacks, walking in place, and sparring with fellow hunters. Dick Brice of La Crosse, Wisconsin, was trapped by the storm on a small island on the Mississippi. Cold and wet, he knew he had to keep warm, and the only thing he could think of was to run in circles, which he did all night. His father and friends, fearing the worst, tried to mount a rescue, but the high winds and waves convinced them the attempt would only result in more deaths. When help arrived the next morning, Dick had worn a circle in the soft ground.

Hunters died heart-achingly close to safety. Two men froze to death only 400 yards from a bonfire they could have seen but were unable to reach. Another hunter wearing a woolen shirt, leather cap, canvas pants, hip boots, sheep-lined vest, a canvas hunting jacket and a football parka froze to death twenty feet from a haystack in which he could have taken shelter. Three St. Paul hunters on Lake Pepin, near Lake City, were heading for shelter when the wind caught and overturned their boat. The three somehow managed to wade ashore, but in the poor visibility failed to spot a farmhouse less than oen hundred yards from where they came ashore. They crept into the only shelter they could find, a culvert, and during the night froze to death.

Ray Sherin's adventures during the storm reads like the script from *The Perils of Pauline,* one of the popular movie serials of the 1930s. Ray, a 14-year-old from Winona and an avid duck hunter, had his sights set on bagging some waterfowl. After a half-day of school that let out at 11:00 A.M. in observance of Armistice Day, Ray and two older friends, Bob Stephens and Cal Wieczorek, headed to the south end of Winona Pool and Ray's father's 16-foot boat powered by a three-horse outboard. They coaxed the engine to life and pointed the small boat north to the southern edge of the Upper Mississippi Wildlife Refuge three miles away. There was a stiff wind blowing, and it had gotten noticeably colder before the boat ride ended. Add the cold rain that dimpled the water and it was duck hunter heaven.

The blinds edging the wildlife refuge—called the "Firing Line" by the locals—were packed with hunters and had been since early morning, so the boys wandered around in search of another likely hunting spot. The wind was howling at a full-blown gale by now, and ducks were rushing past them as if shot from cannons. Ray had a light jacket and gloves. Between the three of them, Bob had the only heavy raincoat. Other supplies included one book of matches.

By late afternoon the three had bagged four ducks in conditions that had gone downhill faster than the stock market in 1929. The three were quite miserable and, if not yet dangerously cold, their hands had grown numb and stiff. They mutually agreed they'd had enough. As if to add an exclamation to their growing misery and concern about finding some warmth and shelter, two older hunters passed them in a small boat and told the boys the worsening conditions had them frightened.

The trio wanted to head home, but in the growing dusk they couldn't determine in which direction that might lie, and they didn't have a compass. The wind had whipped the pool they were on into a fury of whitecaps easily capable of sinking their boat. Within minutes, full dark descended and visibility was halved again when driving snow stung their eyes.

While lost and without a clue as to which direction safety might lie, a skiff appeared out of the dark with four hunters on board. They said they would lead Ray's party to Prairie Island; all the boys had to do was follow. They couldn't. No matter how Ray coaxed the old outboard it failed to start, and Cal and Bob's hands were so cold and stiff they couldn't work the oars. The four hunters quickly disappeared into the whirlwind of snow and spray. Ray later learned their boat capsized and three of the hunters froze to death on the spot. Against long odds, the fourth hunter made it to a small island where he was found the next morning.

The boys finally drifted up to a small sandbar sometime after the hunters left, and Cal and Bob, who were in the bow, leaped ashore and stayed dry. Ray was soaked to the bone by a wave that came over the transom before he could get ashore. The older boys dragged the boat up on the sand and converted it into temporary shelter by turning it over. Ray's clothes were frozen stiff by the time he crawled under the boat and was sandwiched by his two companions who tried to give him some of their body heat.

The wind stalked them throughout the night and the cold continued to sap their strength. The only firewood they scraped together was waterlogged driftwood, and their book of matches died one match at a time in a futile effort to make fire. The only comfort came from Bob's heavy raincoat that was big enough to cover them all. Ray lost feeling in his feet and the two other boys' hands grew useless from the cold. Bob said his hands were all but frozen.

With the coming of daylight, they discovered fifty feet of ice rimmed the sand spit making it difficult and dangerous to get the boat back in the water. They somehow succeeded without getting wet but once back afloat found their hands were too numb to handle an oar. They were blown to the Wisconsin side of the river where they plowed into ice the wind had piled against shore. The impact holed the bow, but their luck held again as the wind drove the boat far enough up on the ice that the hole was out of the water. The friends were once again stranded, this time a hundred yards from shore on ice that couldn't hold their weight and in a boat that couldn't float.

Wind-blown spray enameled their boat in ice and turned their clothes into armor-plated suits. Hypothermia must have become a serious threat as the three crouched in the small boat and wondered what would happen next. An hour after the boat lodged in the ice, a search plane flew over and was soon followed by an Army Corp of Engineer's launch. Rescue and safety was still another hour away because the launch had too deep a draft to reach the boys. A skiff was finally broken out, and the three hunters were brought to the rescue vessel where their frozen clothes and boots were removed and they were wrapped in warm, dry blankets. Ray's dad, leading his own search party, arrived as his son was being taken aboard the army boat.

Bob was in the hospital a week; surprisingly, he suffered no lasting harm to his hands and fingers. Ray's foot had frozen and gangrene set in necessitating partial amputation. During recovery, the 14-year-old's weight plummeted from 143 to 88 pounds. Christmas was less than a week away when the hospital released him. Cal went home the afternoon of the rescue.

Another hunter looking back on that horrible night out on the river gave the following directions for recreating the conditions he endured. Pick a night when the temperature nears zero, dress in light clothes, and set up a big fan outdoors. Cuddle up as close as possible to the fan, turn it on and sit there for the next ten hours. And as the final *pièce de résistance*, select someone to repeatedly douse you in snow, slush, and icy water.

At the Winona airport, Max Conrad stuck the closed sign in the window of the hanger where he ran his flying school and headed home. It was not the kind of night one wanted to be out and about, but his wife had already purchased tickets for a concert at the nearby College of St. Theresa. In spite of the storm, only a few seats were empty when the musician took the stage and began smoothly working his way through a program of light classics. However, several times during the performance wind gusts whipped around the outside of the concert hall with such force it drowned out the young pianist from Milwaukee. At one point, the performer rose from the piano and, with an apologetic shrug, headed for the wings, but the audience wouldn't let the storm upstage the young man and called him back to the piano. It would be a few years yet before candelabra would grace his piano, sequins would weigh down his tuxedo, and the pianist would begin performing under a single name, but even early in his career Walter Liberace knew how to wow a crowd and close a show. In an act of sheer bravado and showmanship, the young man ended the concert with an encore number entitled *The Night Winds*.

As Liberace performed, hundreds of men only a few miles away from the concert hall struggled to stay alive. They walked in circles, hugged their Labs and took them under their coats searching for warmth, beat each other black and blue to keep their blood flowing, crawled under overturned boats, started fires, curled up into fetal positions to conserve body heat, and turned to prayer to survive the night winds.

Rescue operations had already begun that night, but the horrendous conditions made it near impossible to reach the stranded duck hunters. Game wardens and rangers all along the river saved countless lives earlier in the day by urging hunters to leave the river and seek shelter before becoming trapped. Max Conrad spent most of the concert and the night worrying about friends who were in trouble out on the river. The next morning he would mount an extraordinary rescue operation. In the years to come, Max Conrad would become the holder of numerous long-distance, non-stop solo flights; not the least of which included a marathon 7,668-mile flight from North Africa to Los Angeles. He would also become the second man in history to fly solo from New York to Paris. None of those accomplishments would match the incredible bravery or mastery of the air he exhibited the next two days.

Chapter 10

"A Cataclysmic Bang Was Heard Over The Shrieking Wind."

Like everywhere else in the upper Midwest, when the storm front hurtled into Minnesota the weather changed faster than Clark Kent in a telephone booth. It had been a great fall in the "Land of 10,000 Lakes," and no one, including the weather bureau, was running around like Chicken Little warning the populace the sky was falling or at the very least sleet, rain, and better than a foot of snow was going to be falling cross the state. It had been unusually warm and pleasant for weeks. Gardens were still yielding produce, and many flowers continued to bloom.

November temperatures in the state's lower tier of counties continued to bump into the 60s and the annual fall job of putting up storm windows hadn't been given a thought by many homeowners. For that matter, many businesses and homes had not been in a rush to have their winter supply of coal or wood delivered. If you were a football fan, there was another reason to forget about winter being just around the corner. The University of Minnesota football team had beaten Michigan on Saturday, and the Gophers were ranked number one in the country. It was also deer hunting season, which is as solemnly ritualized and as fervently observed in Minnesota and the Upper Midwest as Saint Patrick's Day in New York City. Thousands of hunters donned their seasonal finery and took to the northern woods, and so what if Monday's weather forecast for northern Minnesota called for cooler weather and maybe a chance of snow. Hell, that might improve deer and duck hunting; besides, this was Minnesota where cold weather is relished. Instead, what the state got was a storm that killed forty-nine residents.

The ferocity and suddenness of the storm caught people totally by surprise. A fifteen-year-old paperboy living outside Robbinsdale—

today a suburb of Minneapolis—almost always rode his bike into town to pick up his newspapers. On that Monday afternoon, rain commenced, turned to snow, and built into a full-blown blizzard all within the boy's short peddle to town. The truck that brought the papers to the drop off point never made it, and the young man knew there was no way he could make it home. A friend lived a half-mile away, and the boy waded there through wind-driven snow that cut visibility to a few yards and knee-high drifts that suddenly appeared as if by magic. It took better than a half-hour to reach his friend's house and three days before he could make it back home.

The storm virtually closed every highway and road in the state, and conditions became so bad the Minnesota highway department kept their crews off the roads. The drivers of salt trucks and snowplows waited out the worst of the storm and made ready to counter attack when the weather permitted. A thirty-plus car accident near New Brighton on State Highway 8 left one hundred motorists stranded in the small town or seeking shelter in a nearby farmhouse. The mess began when a car and the White Bear–Stillwater Bus tangled on the highway and three more cars immediately joined in the chain-reaction accident. Unable to see the burgeoning melee through the blizzard, one car after another plowed into the wreckage, including a deputy sheriff's cruiser. The deputy proved to be the most serious of the injured with a deep cut in his lower leg. Ramsey County deputies arrived and transported the injured to hospitals and the uninjured to New Brighton.

Many Minnesota highways turned into linear parking lots as cars were abandoned and quickly covered by snowdrifts. On many roads and streets, car roofs were the only indication of the presence of an automobile, and in a few instances a car's radio antenna sticking up out of a snowdrift was the only clue to what lay beneath the mountain of snow. If a motorist was caught too far from a farmhouse or town, the family car could become a death trap. Along with automobile travel, airlines came to a screeching halt on snow covered runways, and many trains became stranded in drifts. The storm wiped out telephone and telegraph service across much of the state, and electrical power failed when wind, ice, and snow brought down lines and poles.

In many of Minnesota's small towns and farms, the world, for the next two or three days, was reduced down to what you could see, and in the worst of the blizzard that was not much farther than your own outstretched arm. Minnesotans hadn't been this isolated since the pioneer days. As a typical example, the storm shut down Northfield, Minnesota for thirty-six hours. From late Monday afternoon until early Wednesday morning, nothing moved in or through town including buses and passenger trains. More than fifty trucks and a hundred cars were stuck in town, and the drivers and their passengers filled hotels to capacity. With no telephone or telegraph, the town was cut off from the outside world. Up in the state's Iron Range, where grueling winters and bad storms are as common as saunas, old-timers counted the Armistice Day Storm as one of the worst in memory.

⊳✠⊲

The difference between life and death for a Minnesota farmer could come down to whether he had the foresight to string a rope between the house and barn. In the worst of the blizzard, one simply could not see from one to the other, and in whiteout conditions it was easy to become disoriented, stagger off in the wrong direction, and die of cold not forty feet from safety. If farmers got their livestock in the barn before the storm arrived, they survived, if not, they could be wiped out.

Some cattle and sheep froze standing upright, others had their eyes frozen shut by sleet. One farmer literally had to de-ice his cattle. The sleet fell so hard and fast it literally encased his livestock in ice. Luckily, the cattle were close enough to the barn to drive them inside where the ice was knocked off with burlap bags.

Throughout Monday and Tuesday, farmers commonly risked their lives to save their livestock. In Stearns County, farmer George Liedman watched the weather deteriorate into a full-blown blizzard and knew his sixty head of cattle, pastured 3.5 miles from the farmhouse, would likely perish. He ordered his wife to stay indoors and set out on an extraordinary journey. With visibility often reduced to the length of his out-stretched arm and with huge snow drifts barring his way, Liedman still made it to the pasture after two hours of hard labor, but the nearest shelter for his herd lay some distance away at a neighboring farm. Liedman clocked another two hours in the killer storm leading and driving the cattle to the farm. The neighbor urged his friend to stay the night, but the inexhaustible Liedman stayed only long enough to dry his clothes and eat before starting the two-hour trudge home.

The storm consumed a million turkeys in Minnesota that never made it to the Thanksgiving Day table. Across the upper Midwest, an estimated 2.5 million turkeys died inflicting a $12 million financial loss on the region's farmers. The birds died when the quick drop in temperature turned their rain-coated feathers into icy armor or they suffocated when wind-driven snow and ice plugged their nostrils.

On November 11, the workers at Thurnbeck Farm, west of Little Forrest Lake, were deep into the Thanksgiving turkey rush dressing out the birds for the holiday market when the storm struck. Immediately, they turned from slaughtering to saving the birds from the elements. A tractor and trailer crisscrossed fields picking up live gobblers, and when the snow piled too high for the tractor, a horse and wagon continued to pick up turkeys. After the first few passes by the tractor, the birds were often found either buried alive in snow drifts or flash frozen. Workers stuffed the still breathing fowl into barns, sheds, and other outbuildings, and when those filled to bursting, the farmhouse basement became the gobblers' last refuge. The Thurnbeck's lost 2,000 birds. Another farmer lost 1,250 birds out of 3,000 at a cost of $3,000.

Nebraska officials estimated that a quarter of the state's turkey crop died in the storm. In Iowa, thousands of farm-raised Thanksgiving Day birds never made it to the table, and where the state's corn-fed beef were caught in the open, they died in droves. Farther west in the Dakotas, the storm struck with renewed fury. Temperatures fell to ten below zero in Hot Springs, South Dakota, and three below in Custer. Wind-blown snow drifted over roads and piled up in railroad cuts stalling rail and automobile traffic. Livestock out on the open plains, without even the benefit of a river bottom in which to seek shelter from the wind, perished by the hundreds.

Once the livestock was safe or the farmer determined he couldn't do any more for the animals, his mind turned to the other imperative jobs the weather suddenly required of them. It was reported that for those homes without indoor plumbing it often took up to three hours to shovel a path to the outhouse.

Hundreds of bused students found themselves trapped in towns and even in their schools. In St. Cloud, Minnesota alone, more than a hundred students were put up in hotels or taken into private homes until the storm eased and roads were plowed. Students who made it on the bus and out of the school parking lot before the storm reached its full fury discovered the routine and frequently boring ride transformed into the adventure of a lifetime.

When the Sauk Rapids High School let out on Armistice Day, the weather had already turned ugly. The wind-whipped snow took a bite out of the lightly-clothed students as they boarded the bus and set out in the quickly worsening storm. Better than a dozen students still remained on board one bus when the vehicle and the driver reached the end of the same rope. The hand operated windshield wipers, which had difficulty keeping up with an ordinary rainfall, proved near useless in the blizzard, and before long had the driver steering by following telephone poles and sometimes more by memory than sight. When the bus eventually ran off the road, the driver learned from a farmer that a country store was but a quarter-mile up the road. With the driver leading the way and the students linked arm-in-arm—many without hats or mittens—they trudged off into the icy whirlwind. The march of faith ended with the teenagers gathered around the store's glowing wood stove.

The store owners fed their guests, broke out blankets, and at night sent the girls to the cold second floor to share a bed. In the girls' drafty sleeping quarters, a smaller blizzard was created by snow that found its way into the room through the cracks around the windows. The winter castaways' stay lasted three days as students and the owners ate the shelves bare. They passed the time playing cards and telling stories and jokes and grew increasingly tired of waiting and wearing the same clothes day and night.

The bus driver was able to notify a radio station of the bus' location and identify the students who were marooned so parents could be notified their children were safe. It would be Wednesday before a county snow plow finally cleared the road and freed the students.

In the Springfield area, the only person who made it to school on Monday morning was Miss Alta Schweim, the teacher, who was driven to school by her father. No students arrived in the worsening storm, and Miss Schweim found herself marooned without food, water, or lights until Tuesday afternoon. Fortunately, the winter supply of coal had arrived, and she kept warm until rescued.

The nine students who arrived at the one-room school in District #46 in Nicollet County, just north of the little community of New Sweden, on Monday morning would never forget the next 24 hours. Neither would Miss Beatrice Swenson, their twenty-three-year-old teacher. At noon in the quickly worsening weather, Miss Swenson suggested her students eat only part of their packed lunches because it was beginning to look like they wouldn't get home that evening. One of the student's fathers, Mr. Larsen, hitched a team of horses to a sled in the late afternoon and tried to reach the school, but the horses refused to pull into the face of the tempest and Larsen gave up after the wind blew the box off the sled. Other fathers tried to reach the school but couldn't even get out of their own yards. Through the heroic efforts of the local phone company, the school's telephone remained open, and near hysterical parents called to tell their children not to venture outdoors. The nearest home, the Hermanson farm, lay only a quarter-mile east of the one-room school, but in the storm it might as well have been on the other side of the Alps.

The first-year teacher kept the fire roaring in the coal furnace and the children—the oldest, a 13-year-old eighth grader, to the youngest, a 6-year-old first grader—busy with games, music, stories, and riddles. A search turned up one candle which was lit periodically through the night and whenever Miss Swenson went in the basement to stoke the furnace. Coats laid on floors became beds, and everybody got some sleep that night. In the morning, parents checked in by phone with their children who were fine but a little hungry. Mr. Larsen again hitched up his team to the sled and this time reached the school. He took his two children home and dropped Miss

Swenson and the rest of her class off at the Hermanson home where they filled their bellies with piping hot oatmeal. As the day wore on, the other parents shoveled out and reached the Hermanson's and ended their children's great adventure.

The experiences of the first-year teacher and the students in her care inspired a 1957 CBS-TV movie, entitled *Stranded*, with Bette Davis starring in the role of Beatrice Swenson. The half-hour film borrowed heavily from a variety of school-related blizzard experiences and took dramatic license with many factual details.

The telephone proved of immense importance to the parents of the children in District #46's school and to hundreds of other people in Nicollet County. That they had phone service at all and with only brief interruptions during the worst of the storm is testimony to the perseverance and resourcefulness of the employees. Seven operators put in a twenty-four-hour day on Monday handling five to ten times the normal amount of calls. When the electricity failed, a gas-powered generator was located, hauled over, wired into the office, and fired up. When heat in the building went out with the electricity, kerosene stoves were brought in to provide heat. Food and bedding was furnished, and the operators stayed through Monday night connecting the people of Nicollet County with each other.

The phone also brought word of a family tragedy that unfolded just north of New Sweden near Johnson's Corner. On Monday, the Tretbar family car became stuck in a snow drift and Clarence Tretbar, 39, and his wife clearly thought their best chance of survival lay in getting their children—14-year-old Helen and twin brother and sister Robert and Rosemary aged 10—to the nearby G.F. Yetter farm. Clarence got the twins to the farmhouse, but the mother and Helen collapsed in the snow. By the time they were carried into the house, the two lay near death. Yetter called the police in North Mankato who dispatched an ambulance and a state highway department snowplow to punch through the four- and five-foot snow drifts that lay between the town and the victims. The mother and daughter died before the ambulance arrived. A later news story reported the mother and daughter apparently succumbed in part from trying to keep the twins warm by sharing their clothing with the two youngest family members.

The Double Dip, a 24-hour restaurant/truck stop in Mankato, Minnesota, became a port of refuge in Nicollet County on Monday night. By 7:00 P.M. word spread among those who were eating or just taking shelter in the restaurant that the no vacancy sign was showing at every tourist room, hotel, and cluster of tourist cabins in town. The town was jammed with travelers who had the good sense to stop in Mankato rather than wedge their car in a lonely snow bank out in the country. The Double Dip was a friendly beacon in the storm, and many of the motorists naturally gravitated to the truck stop.

The diner's lights failed at 8:00 P.M. followed soon after by the heat. Kerosene lanterns from a local hardware store solved the light problem and helped with the temperature. The Double Dip was wall-to-wall people and one stray dog by 9:00 P.M., and many of the two-legged variety were small children. Using newspapers and the few available blankets, the lone waitress and several parents made up beds for the kids at the back of the restaurant.

The coffee pot was kept in play all night, and when the place started running low on eggs, the short order cook decreed they would be used for pancakes only. Bea Lorenz, the waitress, enlisted the help of truck drivers to wash dishes and even work the counter while she made syrup. Evidently, the wayfarers stayed up all night or snatched a few winks while sitting in a chair. It might have been uncomfortable, but it was much better than getting stranded out in the country and ending up like the lone motorist the highway patrol discovered in a car west of Mankato. He had frozen to death waiting for either help to arrive or the storm to ease.

⛯

In Watkins, Minnesota, west of Minneapolis, the storm cut visibility down to zero and precipitated a train wreck. Passenger Train Number 106, eastbound for the Twin Cities, chugged through Watkins and in the blowing snow missed a track-side signal that should have sent the train onto a siding. Within yards of the town's depot, Number 106 plowed head-on into a slow-moving westbound freight train just leaving the station.

Except for a few adventurous souls, the people of Watkins had holed up in their homes when the blizzard blew into town, and their first inklings of trouble came when the ground shook and a cataclysmic bang was heard over the shrieking wind.

Amanda Ellering of Watkins remembers that by noon power was out, telephones didn't work, and it snowed so heavily she couldn't see her neighbor's house across the street. She vividly recalls, "At about 2:00 p.m. we heard a most awful crash. The house shook, and we couldn't imagine what it was until the train whistles started blowing."[17]

One of the few people out that night was twenty-year-old Wendelin Beckers. He worked the afternoon shift at the Mobil station in town—which sat about a third-of-a-mile from the Soo Line depot—and had been joined by a few friends who were whiling away the blizzard playing cards. The earthquake-like tremors and thunderous wave of sound brought the card game to an abrupt halt. Wendelin and his friends left the warmth of the station and went searching for the source of the loud crash but were driven back by the howling wind. He remembers they had to, "...practically crawl back on our hands and knees to get back to the station. The incredible force of the wind took our breath away. We then wrapped towels or whatever we could around our faces and went out to search again. Visibility wasn't more than eighteen feet, but we finally reached the scene and there discovered the awful truth..."[18]

Beckers, on his second foray, had stumbled across a spur of the railroad and followed the tracks toward the depot where he found the two engines resting on the tracks nose to nose. Steam and smoke rose in the swirling snow, and the impact of the crash jammed one of the train's whistles wide open and led more townspeople to the wreck. The whistle continued to wail for several hours before the boiler emptied of steam. The collision killed the fireman on the freight train, critically injured the engineer, and sent two more railroad workers to the hospital. The passenger train had twenty-two duck hunters onboard who were heading back home to Minneapolis. Back injuries and broken noses were the most common complaints.

Within minutes of the crash and following the sound of the whistle, more townspeople fought their way through the blizzard and joined Wendelin at the site of the crash where they linked hands and formed a human chain to lead the passengers and crew to safety. The injured were rushed to the town doctor, and the rest were taken in by families with the overflow bedded down at city hall. It would be three days before the duck hunters left town.

⚓

If the storm shut down virtually the entire state, it couldn't stop a football game, but maybe it should have. The Winona High School football team and fans traveled to Rochester, Minnesota on Monday morning for a Big Nine Conference afternoon game. By game time with winds gusts approaching fifty mph and the gridiron more a wading pool than a football field, Winona's Coach Loy F. Bowe was more than a little surprised Rochester officials didn't call off the game.

Six hundred spectators braved the weather to at least watch the kick off, but numbers quickly dwindled in the wind-tunnel-force gale and snow pellets that tore at every inch of exposed skin. The wind got so bad the on-field officials had to hold the ball on the ground between plays or it would have blown away. The wind stole or pried loose items of clothing from the spectators, whipping their hats, scarves, and mittens across the field.

At half-time, only 75 people remained on the field, and that included members of both football teams. Those players not in the game forgot rivalry in favor of warmth and huddled together on one side of the field. It was not a day for passing. The reporter for the Winona newspaper wrote, "Winona tried four passes and Rochester two, but they might as well tossed feathers overboard from a stratosphere airliner hoping to hit a barn in Podunk Center."[19]

The game-breaking play and one of the most unusual punts in any football game before or since occurred in the third quarter. Winona punter Bob Harders put his foot into the ball and the wind did the rest. The football left Harders instep and started downfield in a normal trajectory, but as it gained altitude, the ball slowed and then just hung there in mid air as the wind played with it. Talk about hang time. People still in attendance said it stayed in the air like it was a kite. Estimates varied from 10 to 15 seconds before gravity finally started pulling its weight and the ball came down—behind the kicker. If that wasn't bad enough, once on the ground the wind continued to push the ball toward the Rochester goal line. Winona downed the ball before the unthinkable happened, but on the next play Rochester completed what the wind had started and punched the ball into the end zone for six points. Final score: Winona 6, Rochester 13. By the end of the game and with home only lying 45 miles away, the Winona team and its fans were stranded for the night in Rochester.

The storm played havoc with rural and small town Minnesota, but it didn't cut the Twin Cities any slack. A 24-hour record snowfall buried the Twin Cities under 16.8 inches of the white stuff which the wind then piled into drifts as high as five feet. Overnight, the thermometer sank to six degrees above zero. With winds swirling through downtown Minneapolis and Saint Paul that topped out at over 60 mph, the wind-chill factor plummeted to life threatening extremes, all of which turned the neighboring cities into a frozen nightmare.

White-outs and snow drifts slowed traffic and then stopped it. Car tires packed snow and slush into the trolley tracks, and freezing cold temperatures turned the slush to cement which derailed the cars and halted trolley service citywide by noon. At one point, forty street cars were off their tracks in Minneapolis. Trains stopped, the airport shutdown, cabs were pulled off the streets, and buses sat in their terminals.

When offices and businesses closed and emptied thousands out onto downtown streets, it just compounded the cities' problems. A new wave of cars became stuck in snow banks and unplowed roads and were quickly abandoned. Many of the cars would remain buried in the snow for up to five days. Tow truck operators couldn't keep up with business. They left on the first call and never returned to the garage as they tried to pull one car after another out of snow banks and ditches. Most tow truck drivers finally just gave up and went home and waited the weather out.

In St. Paul, police cars became ambulances and transported half-a-dozen expectant mothers to the hospital. Across town in

Minneapolis, a few stranded but ingenious citizens went to the hospital and when a call came in for an ambulance run that passed close to their homes, the stranded begged a ride and usually got it.

The storm marooned thousands in downtown Minneapolis, and when hotel rooms quickly sold out, people camped in lobbies, hallways, hotel dining rooms, or spent the night in the office. The proprietor of a downtown clothing emporium bedded down in his store on a deep pile of overcoats. Fifty people spent the night in John Swanson and Sons grocery store on East Twenty-Fifth Street.

Pubs and bars in Minneapolis and St. Paul, as well as all across Minnesota, became impromptu emergency shelters. Al's Bar in St. Louis Park, the first bar west of the Minneapolis city limits, was always jammed during Minneapolis elections, when, by law, city bars had to close, and during inclement weather because the watering hole maintained a strict policy of never closing under either of the above conditions. The stranded and Al's habituates struggled into bar throughout the day on Monday as if it was an oasis in the middle of the Sahara—they crawled across automobiles buried up to their roofs in snow rather than burning sands—and commenced a three-day party.

Travelers stuck in the Minneapolis bus station were looking forward to a long, boring, uncomfortable night spent in the depot when the station's loudspeaker announced that the Gaiety Burlesque Theatre was putting on a free show for anyone who could get to the theatre. Since it was directly across the street, there was an immediate rush for the door and a human chain was formed to get everyone safely across the street and into the show.

Unbelievably, in the two cities where services simply froze up and movement of any kind over the next several days became difficult if not impossible, the Tribune's newsboys apparently found a way to deliver their papers. Paperboys and other winter bike riders were known to wrap ropes around the rear tires of their bicycles to get better traction in the snow, but by Tuesday morning drifts were so deep most bikes were left at home in favor of walking the route. Some had friends help them, but invariably the papers were delivered late and there were some self-centered, unappreciative subscribers who chewed out their paperboy for not getting the paper to them at the usual time. One former paperboy remembers the real miracle was that the trucks carrying the papers to the route carriers somehow got through over unplowed roads often clogged with abandoned cars.

A few weeks after the storm, the Tribune Newspapers awarded a Certificate of Merit to newsboys who braved the elements and succeeded in delivering papers to homes on their routes. The Certificate of Merit reads, "Know all men by these presents that, in the face of actual physical danger and with great bravery and determination, and that on the day of the worst blizzard the Northwest has ever known, the Armistice Day Blizzard of November 1940, [name] did perform his duty in a courageous, noble manner, in delivering the Tribune Newspapers to his subscribers against great difficulties."[20]

Lake Superior also reeled under the impact of the inland hurricane, but tragedy was averted on the largest of the Great Lakes because storm warnings went up early and were heeded. On Armistice Day 1940, the barometric pressure at Duluth, Minnesota, fell to 28.66," the lowest ever recorded before or since at this great inland port. The storm's southwest to northeast track also meant that the western end of Lake Superior would feel the brunt of the whirlwind very early on Monday.

The U.S. Weather Bureau in Duluth posted storm warnings for Lake Superior as early as 6:30 A.M. Unlike the Great Storm of 1913 when captains with a lifetime of sailing experience thought they knew more about the weather than any desk-bound meteorologist and ignored the postings, this time, ships stayed in port. Even a ship's home office was getting in the act. The *Edmund W. Mudge* was just finishing taking on a load of ore when the office in Cleveland called and ordered Captain W. Ross Maitland to remain in port until the storm passed. Other captains made up their own minds to delay departure and ride out the blow in the protected waters of the Duluth, Minnesota's and Superior, Wisconsin's twin harbors. At least one ship that put out into the big lake before the storm warnings went up felt the first great push of the wind and quickly turned back to safety.

Several ships were nearing the twin harbors at the west end of Lake Superior when the cyclone raced out of the southwest to test ships and seamen. The crew of the *Crescent City* was looking forward to at least a few hours of leave as they neared the Minnesota port with a deck load of new cars destined for Duluth dealerships. Thoughts of leave were forgotten as the storm overtook the *Crescent City* and tried to swallow the ship whole. Gigantic waves roared down on the steamer, covered her steering pole, and climbed over the bow inundating the deck in a rush of water. Captain Harold B. McCool knew the ship's continued existence depended on keeping it headed into the monstrous seas because it was a dead certainty that if one of the rolling avalanches of water pushed the *Crescent City* broadside to a following wave and the ship fell into a trough, he and the crew were doomed. So it was one of the least of his worries that morning as he watched the big waves board his ship and like buccaneers steal away the cargo of automobiles. The *Crescent City* reached Duluth that day, but that city's new-car dealers didn't have a lot to show for the ship's safe arrival.

And finally, Monday November 11, 1940 marked the day ship-to-shore radios came of age on the Great Lakes. The Hageman brothers of Lorain, Ohio, owners of a small telephone company became interested in radio broadcasting and formed the Lorain County Radio Corporation in 1928.

After several less than spectacular projects sputtered and died, the brothers looked into ship-to-shore radio and installed the first unit, a device the size of a small closet, on the steamer *William C. Atwater* in 1933. When the *Atwater's* captain was severely injured in an onboard accident and the ship's medic was talked through emergency procedures by a doctor hurriedly summoned to the company's wireless switchboard in Lorain, Ohio, the value of ship-to-shore radio was obvious. Many shipping companies and captains had radiotelephones installed in their ship's pilothouses, and by 1940 they were standard equipment on many lake freighters. All calls had to go through the company's on-shore radio switchboards, and to achieve complete coverage throughout the Great Lakes, the company built stations at Port Washington, Wisconsin and Duluth, Minnesota.

On Armistice Day, calls for assistance from ships in trouble poured into the Lorain office and were quickly forwarded to the nearest coast guard station. The company usually manned the switchboard with two operators a shift, but as the weather worsened and radio traffic increased, more operators were called into work. By the end of the day, the company had its busiest day ever with five operators handling almost 500 ship-to-shore telephone messages. Tuesday was nearly as busy as skippers all over the lakes reported to company offices and owners that their ships had weathered the storm.

TUESDAY

Chapter 11

"A Near Miraculous Crossing."

There were few optimists left in South Haven, Michigan by Tuesday afternoon. On Monday, two South Haven commercial fishing tugs, the *Indian* and the *Richard H.*, had put out into Lake Michigan and had not been seen since. When the two boats disappeared into the storm's roiling maw, four men from the South Haven Coast Guard Station launched a 36-foot motor surfboat and went looking for the fishermen. If it seemed an impossible—even foolhardy—quest, so be it. The impossible had long been and is still expected of and performed daily by the U.S. Coast Guard. On Monday, the surfboat had no more than cleared the dock before it, too, disappeared, and neither boat nor crew had been seen or heard from in better than 24-hours.

South Haven Coast Guard Captain William Fisher still held out some hope for the *Indian*. It had a diesel engine, an experienced crew, and just the past year the boat had been caught out on the lake in a similar storm and had ridden it out by heading for Chicago. The captain was less sanguine about the *Richard H.* It was not only a smaller boat and underpowered, it had gone to sea with a less experienced crew.

The loved ones of those who sailed on the *Indian* simply could not believe the boat and crew were lost. In a lifetime of fishing, these Great Lakes fishermen had survived other bad storms, and more than once they brought the battered little fishing tug back to dock when others had abandoned all hope. They couldn't be gone. But if the lake hadn't taken, them where were they?

At about 6:00 P.M., a Coast Guard shore party walking the beach between Grand Haven and Holland came upon the broken and battered remains of the *Indian*. Debris from the tug was strewn for four miles along the beach, and the wreckage from the tug's

Wreckage of the Indian.
Photo courtesy of the Michigan Maritime Museum.

pilothouse came to rest in Little Pigeon Creek, ten miles north of Holland. The imprint of the Berger Boat Company on the pilothouse positively identified the boat as the *Indian*.

The Church of the Epiphany in South Haven announced a Wednesday morning requiem mass would be said for the twelve missing crewmembers of the *Indian, Richard H.,* and the Coast Guard surfboat.

Two of the surfboat's crew, Jesse Meeker and Ken Courtright, were married, and their wives had kept a lonely vigil since their husbands' departure. After twenty-seven straight hours, the women must have felt like they were waiting on the edge of a bottomless, emotional abyss. At about the same time that the wreckage of the *Indian* was discovered, the wives received a phone call from Chicago. Their husbands were calling.

After a twenty-seven-hour ordeal, the South Haven surfboat completed a near miraculous crossing of Lake Michigan. Boatswain's Mate Dudley, as quoted by UPI, dismissed the feat with a modest, "We knew we had a stout little boat and a good motor and a capable crew."[21] In a more sober assessment of what he and his crew had experienced, Dudley, a sixteen-year veteran of the U.S. Coast Guard, told the *Ludington Daily News*, "It was the worst storm on the lake that I've ever seen, and I've been in plenty of them."[22]

After leaving South Haven, Dudley steered the surfboat to the southwest and searched for any sign of the two fishing tugs or the men who sailed them. They sighted nothing over the next five hours except towering waves, some of which topped out at over forty feet. All the while, the "stout little boat" was in danger of being hammered into the lake like a ten-penny nail into a two-by-four by the four-story-tall waves. In danger of going down, the boatswain's mate decided to break off the search and head for safety, but he and the crew knew they couldn't return to South Haven because to move at right angles to the huge waves would be suicidal. Instead, they headed into the wind and made for Chicago at two to three mph. The men went without sleep Monday night as they chipped ice off the boat and flirted with doom when the boat twice threatened to capsize.

The battered, storm-tossed boat and crew motored into Chicago harbor a little before 6:00 p.m. The surfboat was rimmed in ice and the crew was hungry, tired, and black and blue from the cold and being thrown around the boat's small cockpit. The men were noticeably shivering, and in an understatement worthy of Boatswains' Mate Elmer Dudley himself, the *South Haven Daily Tribune* reported the men appeared, "slightly weathered."[23] The surfboat had left South Haven with a full load of fuel—200 gallons. When Dudley turned off the engine in Chicago 20 gallons were left in the tank.

The Coast Guard men were completely played out and ached for sleep, and after a quick call to South Haven, they tumbled into bunks and temporary oblivion. Their first thoughts on awaking were to immediately head back to South Haven. The men had a feeling they might be needed there.

The forty-five crewmen and four passengers aboard the car ferry *City of Flint* were warm and well fed Tuesday morning but probably hadn't gotten much sleep the previous night. With the waves constantly breaking against the hull, it must have been like living inside a steel drum. Even though the ship rested on the sandy lake bottom barely a football field from shore, each big wave rocked the ship back and forth. By morning, the decks and superstructure had been turned into a strange wonderland by freezing spray. Every inch of exposed deck, railing, stairway, cable, and piece of deck equipment had been thickly slathered in ice by wind-driven spray and waves that exploded against the side of the ship, wet everything on deck, and froze as it ran off. It left the ship looking like a crew of crazed cake decorators had been loosed on the car ferry overnight.

Leland H. Kent, Marine Superintendent for the Pere Marquette Railway Company was on the beach early Tuesday to assess the situation. As he testified later at a U.S. Coast Guard inquiry, he was not encouraged by what he saw. He said, "The major point from my point of view was that here was a boat just managing to get by. The gangway had practically caved in on the starboard side... For quite a period of time it looked like we were going to have to take the crew off."[24]

The Marine Superintendent was also concerned that the wind might shift direction and come out of the northwest, which could have driven the ferry against the breakwater. Kent also thought the ship could have filled up with sand if the wind rotated to the northwest. Kent recalled, "As it was we just got by and got it off in time."[25]

The coast guard had been on the beach all night, and with first light Tuesday morning fired a line to the *City of Flint* and rigged a breeches buoy from ship to shore. In many emergency situations, the device had proven to be the only safe method of rescuing crew and passengers from shipwrecks or stranded vessels lying close to shore that because of surf conditions couldn't be reached by boat. The breeches buoy is essentially a life ring with a pair of cut-off trousers sewn into the ring. The breeches buoy is attached by lines and a pulley to an overhead cable that has been fired by a Lyle Cannon to the stranded ship. Once the cable has been secured at either end, the breeches buoy is mounted on the cable, and by means of ropes tied to the life ring, it is pulled back and forth from ship to shore. A passenger literally steps into the canvas breeches like he or she was going to wear them and holds on to the lines that go overhead to the pulley and is pulled to shore. The problem here is—as anyone who has ever hung washing on a clothes line knows—the line, no matter how tightly stretched, sags in the middle and commonly dunks the passenger in the water. All the necessary equipment—buoy, lines, pulley, Lyle Cannon, and even a tripod over which the line on shore could be strung in hopes of reducing the passenger's baptism from full to partial—is stored on a wheeled cart that guardsmen pull along the shore until they are opposite a stranded vessel. The breeches buoy's effective working range is 350 yards.

With the breeches buoy rigged and ready to go, crewman Ernest Detolowski, a Ludington native son, slipped a note from the captain into his pocket, put on the canvas pants, and with the men on shore heaving away began his short, but dramatic, journey. The Coast Guard and the unfortunate Detolowski quickly discovered that when you added the effects of the ship's rocking motion to the natural sag in the buoy's overhead line, it made for an unpleasant and dangerous journey. Ernest was not only repeatedly doused in the lake but dragged through a good part of it before reaching the beach. The seaman arrived on the beach considerably less well off than when he left the ship and was sent to the hospital. The message from the captain Detolowski had started the trip with had gone AWOL during one of his frequent immersions.

The word persistence should appear somewhere on the U.S. Coast Guard emblem. When the first trip via breeches buoy didn't go exactly as planned, they requested that a second sailor be selected for transportation. The records don't reveal if this second crewman volunteered or was ordered into the breeches buoy. Like the first man, the second also arrived more dead than alive and had to be taken to the hospital. The captain, tired of seeing his crewmen landed like hooked tuna, ordered a moratorium on breeches buoy trips for his crew. The device was then employed in sending a telephone line, insulators, and a coil of wire to the ship. The latter two items were needed to get the ship's radio working.

The Coast Guard had also hauled a surf boat to the beach in case it was needed, which occurred at 12:30 in the afternoon when the car ferry reported a man overboard. The oar-powered surf

First seaman from the City of Flint to arrive on the shore
via the breeches buoy is helped up the beach.

Photo by Harold Holmes from the David K. Petersen Maritime Collection.

boat was launched and found a life-vest-jacketed body floating near
the stranded ship, but it hadn't come from the *City of Flint*. The
stenciling on the vest identified the body as a sailor off the *William
B. Davock*. The dead sailor was the first indication that the *Davock*
might have gone down in the storm. Within a half-hour, several
more bodies, all wearing life preservers stenciled with the name *W.
B. Davock*, had been carried to shore by wind and waves.

If anyone needed further proof that the war in Europe was
slowly spreading its tentacles even into the Great Lakes, one did
not have to look further than Ludington Harbor on this Armistice
Day. Seven new U.S. Naval Reserve sub-chasers on their way from
a shipyard in Sturgeon Bay, Wisconsin, to the Brooklyn Navy Yard
where they would be armed and outfitted for Atlantic patrol duty
were caught in the harbor when the storm struck. Even though
they were in protected waters, the 75- to 110-foot-long ships were
tossed around like corks. At one time or another through the night,

it looked like two of the ships might go to the bottom of the harbor, and although the ships remained afloat, they all suffered heavy damage. A.E. Schlobohm, serving on one of the sub-chasers as a ship's cook, second class said of the experience, "I've traveled the ocean and been in storms before, but this one, on an inland lake, makes the others seem insignificant."[26] Jack Terrell, a boatswain, first class in the Naval Reserve added, "[I] only thought things like this happened in the movies but found out different."[27]

On Tuesday, the crews had been on duty for 24 hours keeping the pumps operating, assessing damage, repairing what they could, and chipping or hosing away the ice that encrusted each of the sub-chasers. It would be Friday before the seven vessels sailed back to Sturgeon Bay where they would be surveyed and fully repaired. Two of the sub-chasers took such a severe pounding they wouldn't make it to the Brooklyn Navy Yard until the spring of 1941.

During the night, the crew of *Car Ferry 21* popped their ship free from the pilings in which it had wedged its bow when she came careening into harbor late Monday afternoon. The ship was eased into slip number 3, off-loaded, had its damage assessed, and then began loading cars for a return trip to Manitowoc, Wisconsin. Early Tuesday morning, with the storm still raging across the width and breadth of Lake Michigan, the car ferry left Ludington breakwater, passed within a stone's throw of the stranded *City of Flint #32*, and pointed her bow into the heavy seas.

Chapter 12

"Their Salvation Now Rested in the Hands of Strangers."

From the moment the *Novadoc* struck at around 9:00 P.M. Monday night and through most of Tuesday, the broken ship and her trapped crew were subjected to a horrific watery bombardment. Huge rollers broke over the vessel in explosions of foam and spray that shot high into the air completely obliterating any view of the ship from those on shore. Someone took an 8 mm motion-picture camera to the beach on Tuesday and recorded the waves crashing into and over the grounded ship. Whether watching from the beach in 1940 or via the film sixty years later, one would almost swear the *Novadoc* was taking direct hits from 1,000-pound bombs. As each oncoming wave collided with the *Novadoc*, the broken ship disappeared in a boiling cloud of what looked like sea and smoke, and no matter how many times the film is watched, there is still that small degree of surprise when the foam and high-flying spray momentarily subsided to reveal the Novadoc had not been blown to smithereens. On board the ship, each thunderous impact chipped away at the wreck and shook the crew.

Muted by heavy cloud cover, dawn came slowly on Tuesday morning. With the first glimpse outside, the crew discovered the ship's lifeboats were gone, swept away by the storm. The first mate—in spite of suffering a deep facial gash from flying glass when the pilothouse windows blew in—wanted to swim to shore carrying a line, but Captain Steip vetoed the idea: their salvation now rested in the hands of strangers. According to Belcher, the crew didn't see anyone on the beach until three men appeared about 9:30 A.M. Wanting to let them know survivors were on board, Belcher ripped a sheet from a bed and waved it out a porthole. Belcher and the rest of the crew assumed the waving sheet had gotten the attention of the

Waves batter the Novadoc on Tuesday.

Photo by Harold Holmes from the David K. Petersen Collection.

trio because they soon left and returned with a dozen more men. In a letter to the Great Lakes Shipwreck Museum at Whitefish Point, Michigan, Belcher says the crew fired off distress rockets throughout the day and even tried firing a line to shore, but it fell short. The stranded men watched throughout the day as more and more people gathered on Juniper Beach and began a vigil that continued until the crew was rescued.

The events surrounding the eventual rescue of the *Novadoc* crew would range from high drama to low comedy. Over the next 24 hours, the public's displeasure with the U.S. Coast Guard's inaction ignited a controversy that continued long after the November storm and resulted in a Coast Guard Board Investigation. The weather was a significant contributor to the approaching confusion and controversy, but in the end human inexperience as well as lack of leadership and clear thinking trumped Mother Nature.

The conditions on shore opposite the *Novadoc* on Tuesday morning were extraordinarily nasty. William Krewell, the light keeper at Little Sable Point Light Station estimated the winds at

75 mph with the air filled with blowing sand. To look directly into the wind was like having your face sandblasted. The hurricane force winds blowing from the southwest had piled up water on the Michigan shoreline and raised the lake level along the eastern shore as much as 6 to 8 feet. This rise in water level wiped out beaches in the Little Sable Point area and sent waves crashing against the steep dunes that normally sat dozens of yards back from the shore. Increasing the discomfort was the blowing snow which at times obliterated visibility and falling temperatures that combined with the cyclonic winds to send the wind chill index to cryogenic levels. One Coast Guardsman reported being blown backward off the top of dunes overlooking beach. Dr. Lewis B. Munger of Hart, Michigan, went to the shore to view the wreck on Tuesday and later testified regarding the conditions he found on Juniper Beach. He said, "I could hardly stand up because of the wind, and the sand was blowing in my eyes that I could hardly see. I tried to walk along the beach but the water was so high that it was impossible."[28]

When Chief Boatswain A.E. Kristofferson, Commander of the Ludington Station, received word of the possible grounding of a ship near Little Sable Point, he grabbed a couple of men and left for the lighthouse where he arrived just before midnight. In the wind and dark, it proved impossible to conduct any beach patrol or search, and he left for Ludington by 3:00 A.M. A crew from the Grand Haven Coast Guard Station had been dispatched to Little Sable Point with a beach cart and a motor surfboat. They pulled into the lighthouse at 7:00 A.M. after an all night drive and were met by detachments from the White River and Muskegon stations.

In a Report of Assistance prepared by Surfman Roland D. Ericson of the Grand Haven Station, he wrote, "Men were immediately placed on the beach to make a patrol between Little Sable Light Station and Pentwater Lifeboat Station. After covering a distance of approximately one mile, the grounded steamer *Novadoc* was sighted. From all appearances, it first appeared as if no one was living aboard the grounded steamer. However, after awhile it was discovered that some of the men were still alive in the pilothouse and in no immediate danger."[29]

There is some question as to when Commanding Officer Kristofferson first learned of survivors aboard the *Novadoc*. During the official investigation into handling of the rescue operation, he testified that he was not informed of survivors aboard the wreck until Wednesday morning. However, Kristofferson arrived back in the Pentwater area shortly after the *Novadoc* was discovered (around 9:30 A.M.) with Boatswain Richard Herline (Retired) and immediately made for the beach where the *Novadoc* had grounded. From the end of a road, he and Boatswain Herline walked to the shore where they met and talked with two men from the Muskegon Coast Guard Station who were standing watch over the wreck. In a report to Chicago District Commander dated November 16, 1940, Kristofferson wrote, "They informed us that one man had seen someone waving from a porthole. It was blowing a whole gale, and the flying sand made it impossible to look straight at the vessel for more than a moment at a time."[30]

One is left wondering whether the commanding officer later discounted the sighting because of the weather conditions or utterly dismissed it as wishful thinking. Several civilians reported seeing a sheet or rag being waved from the ship on Tuesday morning, yet no one ever mentioned seeing distress flares during the day which Belcher recalls were fired off several times. It's hard to imagine, but apparently the weather was so bad even distress flares could not be seen.

What seems inconceivable is that signs of life would be observed on board the wreck from sometime early Tuesday morning yet Chief Boatswain Kristofferson, the officer in command of the U.S. Coast Guard operations in the area, would not have been informed that men or signs of life were seen on the wreck until Wednesday morning.

According to the Record of Proceedings of a Board Investigation held in Pentwater, Michigan, by the U.S. Coast Guard to examine the facts and circumstances connected with the loss of lives from the steamships *Novadoc*, *W.B. Davock*, and *Anna C. Minch*, the first positive evidence of survivors on the *Novadoc* occurred when flares and fires were seen on the ship the night of November 12. That makes a twelve-hour gap from the time Belcher was observed waving a sheet out of a porthole and the first officially recorded sighting of the stranded ship's crew.

After observing the *Novadoc* on Tuesday morning and talking with the two men from Muskegon, Kristofferson returned to his car where he met Chief Boatswain Alfred M. Anderson of the Grand Haven Station. Kristofferson felt it necessary he return to Ludington so he could directly monitor the car ferry situation, and in this face-to-face meeting placed Anderson in charge of the *Novadoc* rescue mission. The only problem was Anderson came away from the meeting thinking he had received no such order. He later admitted under oath he was the senior man on the scene after Chief Boatswain Kristofferson left for Ludington. Anderson also testified he did not see any life aboard the *Novadoc* until 8 P.M. Tuesday when the crew of the vessel fired a distress signal. He did admit other men had seen signs of life on the ship earlier that day. One can only wonder if that information was forwarded to Kristofferson. There is no record of any member of the Coast Guard spotting a distress signal coming from the *Novadoc* other than the one seen at 8:00 P.M. Tuesday night.

The beach cart with its breeches buoy equipment became another point of contention between the Coast Guard and the public. The Grand Haven Coast Guard contingent got the beach apparatus cart within three-quarters of mile of the wreck when they ran out of road. The road ended on the land side of a large dune. On any other day of the year there would have been a sizeable stretch of sand and beach on the dune's reverse side before one dipped a toe in water, but not on Tuesday, November 12, 1940. The storm surge had completely covered the beach and had Lake Michigan lapping at the very foot of the dunes. Area residents offered both a tractor and a team of horses to haul the cart through the dunes to the site of the wreck and even volunteered to manhandle the various pieces of equipment to the beach. The Coast Guard refused all offers of assistance and apparently neither asked locals if they knew of any road that could get their equipment closer to the site of the grounding nor went in search of one themselves.

Chief Boatswain Kristofferson had concluded it would have been impossible to use the breeches buoy even if they had gotten it to the scene of the grounding. Shooting a line to the ship, in Kristofferson's opinion, would only further endanger the Novadoc crew because anyone on board who tried to retrieve and anchor a line on a ship that was constantly awash in huge waves would have perished. There were many among the public and the Coast Guard who were on the beach that day and agreed with the Chief Boatswain.

William F. Barnhart, machinists mate first class, with 31 years in the Coast Guard thought the breeches buoy, if it could have been strung from ship to shore would have only added to the disaster. At the Board Investigation Barnhart testified, "My opinion is that if we would have fixed up the breeches buoy, we would have drowned every man that would have gotten into the breeches buoy because I don't think we could stretch the line out of the water, which would have necessitated pulling the survivors to shore under water."[31] Obviously drowning a survivor in order to save them is a less than perfect rescue plan, but the communities of Ludington and Pentwater were afloat with experienced Great Lakes sailors who bristled at the idea that no one was doing anything to rescue the trapped sailors. At least a few, including John Peterson, the *Novadoc* crewman who had so far barely escaped with his life when the ship struck Juniper Beach, thought the breeches buoy could be made to work.

Another man who was less than content with the efforts of the U.S. Coast Guard was area fisherman Clyde Cross. Born in 1908 on Beaver Island, Clyde came from a well-known commercial fishing family and had a lifetime of Great Lakes sailing experience under his belt. He was one of nine brothers, all of whom made a living wresting fish from the big lake. Clyde operated out of Pentwater and was master and owner of the *Three Brothers II*, an old, small, and nearly clapped out fishing tug powered by an equally old engine that began life in a Buick automobile.

The oldest commercial fishing tug in the region, the *Three Brothers II* had been tested and tempered by Lake Michigan for 36 years. His longtime crew consisted of Gustavo "Corky" Fisher and Joe "Tontoni" Fountain. Not a lot is known about Joe, but "Corky" was a well-liked local character with more personality than you could fit in a 256-pound frame. The muscular fire plug lived life with an eye for adventure and had driven trucks loaded with explosives in Texas, sailed in the treacherous Alaskan waters, and barnstormed with airplanes.

On Tuesday, Clyde and "Corky" drove to the beach and visited the site of the wreck. The two fishermen arrived about 1:30 P.M. and found about twenty people watching the waves pound away at the *Novadoc* but could not find anyone there from the Coast Guard. On the drive out to Juniper Beach, Clyde had picked up two Coast Guardsmen about two miles from the wreck. The hitchhikers unaccountably chose to stay in the car when Fisher and Cross walked to the beach to view the stranded ship and then rode back to Pentwater with the two fishermen. After the visit to the beach, Cross offered the use of his boat to the Chief Boatswain Anderson and told him he could arrange to have 75 men on hand, at any time of his choosing, to carry the beach cart and breeches buoy to the site of the wreck. All Anderson had to do was say when. The Coast Guard turned down both offers.

By Tuesday evening, Cross could think of nothing but saving the *Novadoc's* stranded crewmen. He talked with his crew and paced the shoreline and finally told Fisher and Fountain he couldn't bear the thought that men were still alive out there and someone had to step forward and attempt a rescue. Clyde Cross would not sleep Tuesday night; his mind was with the *Novadoc* crew.

Grumbling continued to spread among the locals as the Coast Guard made no attempt to rescue the *Novadoc's* crew and gave no indication of even preparing a rescue operation. People wanted to see a surfboat brought to the beach and a try made to reach the *Novadoc*. Others thought a powered surfboat should be launched at Pentwater and sent to the aid of the crew. Most experienced sailors and Coast Guardsmen felt it would have been suicidal to try and launch the surfboat from the beach or attempt to motor any vessel out of Pentwater harbor during the daylight hours on Tuesday. Veteran seamen knew that the huge waves climbing over the piers guarding Pentwater's harbor entrance would have instantly thrown a surfboat onto one of the rocky arms and destroyed it. Many in the area continued to lose patience with the Coast Guard and its local leadership. Where were the unsinkable surfboats, the specialized gear, and for that matter, the men who spent years training to use them? The men on the *Novadoc* could well have been asking the same questions.

For most of Tuesday, the only comfort the *Novadoc's* crew could find in their present situation was the small crowd of men and women who wandered down to the beach to catch a glimpse of the stranded vessel and then, in the simple act of hanging around and becoming a witness to the unfolding event, struck a tenuous solidarity with the men held hostage by circumstance and nature.

The grounded *Novadoc* lay low in the water. The bow had some freeboard, but the rest of ship aft the bow was so low it was nearly awash. After better than twelve hours of pounding by the waves, the hull lay almost parallel to the shore with the rear of the ship tilting slightly toward deeper water. Somebody in the forward part of the ship found an aluminum pail that was instantly turned into a fireplace. The crewmen kept busy for a while breaking up the captain's furniture and even wood paneling from his office walls into small enough pieces to fit into the pail and feed the fire. Those in the forward section knew someone in the stern was alive because they kept seeing a light in the porthole.

The crew in the aft section of the wreck was trapped in a sink of misery. The men were constantly up to their knees in freezing water, and many felt they were in danger of drowning. All day Tuesday, everybody but the injured John Peterson bailed continuously as water poured into the cabin and the seas threatened to tear the aft superstructure apart and wash the men into Lake Michigan. Throughout the day Tuesday, they heaved bucketfuls of water out of portholes only to have wind and wave pour it right back in.

With the arrival of darkness on Tuesday evening, the crew, suffering from hunger, cold, and exposure, settled in for another disheartening night wondering when and if they were ever going to be rescued. They took some encouragement from the bonfire the small crowd on the beach had started and kept blazing all night. It meant somebody was out there and somebody cared.

One wonders whether David Prentice could enjoy the irony of his predicament. Had Prentice been just a few pounds lighter, he wouldn't have been on the *Novadoc*. He had signed up for the Royal

Canadian Navy, but after taking his induction physical Prentice was told he was too heavy. The young man was sent home to lose a few pounds, and he decided to shed the weight working a few runs on the *Novadoc*. He hadn't bargained for a crash diet!

The voyage served as a rude introduction to the trade for two young men from Elmvale, Ontario. Douglas Houden, 18, served as a watchman while 16-year-old Everett Turner was rated a deckhand. A sailor's very first voyage is always a standout in one's memory, but when the trip ends in a shipwreck, it makes for an indelible experience.

Throughout Tuesday night, *Novadoc's* crew knew their situation was growing ever more precarious. The ship continued to shudder and shift under the pounding waves, and the men knew the wreck could easily slip into deeper water. Dick Sempell, the *Novadoc's* first mate said of that night, "A sudden shift in the wind would have finished the boat for good."[32] Years later, Lloyd Belcher clearly recalled how discouraged the crew was after waiting all day for help to arrive and then facing another uncertain night on the wreck. He remembered the long, cold, dark hours and said, "The night seemed like weeks as there was nothing to do but wait until help arrived."[33]

When word of the *Novadoc's* grounding reached loved ones in Canada, it struck emotional bruises that still had not completely healed. The first news to arrive declared the ship lost but that was shortly followed with the announcement the *Novadoc* had struck a shoal and broken in two. Once again, the waiting and praying began, for this latest crisis marked the fourth time in four years the *Novadoc* had been reported missing. And no matter how many times one hears devastatingly bad news and then learns it's false, the experience does not create emotional calluses.

Chapter 13

"The Bodies Floated to Shore Intermingled with the Wreckage."

On Tuesday morning, the airwaves, telephone lines, and wire services hummed with the news and rumors of ships reported aground or lost to the storm. There was also great concern about the many ships that were overdue in reaching port. As the hours dragged by and the vessels failed to appear, their names were added to the growing list of the missing and overdue. The battered ships still out on the lake and struggling to reach a safe anchorage not only had to cope with raging seas, blinding snow, and wind, but in many cases without the usual navigational aids. From the Straits of Mackinac to Grand Haven, buoys, lighted bell buoys, range lights, fog signals, and radio beacons had been carried away, damaged, or destroyed.

Rumor and uncertainty quickly gave way to grim facts from the U.S. Coast Guard and the many volunteers, including twenty-five young men from the Civilian Conservation Corp, patrolling the eastern shoreline of Lake Michigan on Tuesday morning. Debris from the various disasters and near disasters littered more than 200 miles of beach. The first body from the *William B. Davock* was discovered shortly after noon and, at first, was thought to have come from the car ferry *City of Flint*. Within thirty minutes, six more bodies were found along the shore north of the north pier at Ludington where coast guard crews and volunteers had the melancholy task of collecting them.

The dungaree and life-preserver-clad bodies floated to shore intermingled with debris that hadn't gone down with the ship. The wreckage came ashore in a remarkable variety of shapes and sizes from good-sized chunks of life boats and recognizable pieces of the superstructure down to odd scraps of wood that hinted at what they could have been before the cataclysm intermingled with mulch-sized pieces which might have been wood paneling or furniture that had been instantly transmogrified into chaff as the ship broke up. All of it either ended up curling in the surf or lay on the sand where the waves had thrown it.

There was the sad irony of empty life rings and life jackets occupying the same beach as the recently drowned. Some of the bodies lay well up on the beach, carried there by the pounding surf, while others tentatively nudged the beach as if the lake hadn't quite decided whether or not to give up the dead. All the bodies were rigid and cold.

The *Great Lakes Journal* reported that much of the wreckage that drifted ashore from the stricken vessels was carted off by beachcombers and souvenir hunters before the Coast Guard patrols had a chance to examine it. Even when a beach patrol was the first to come across wreckage and took efforts to gather and hide the debris for later study before moving on down the beach in search of bodies and more wreckage, it wasn't safe. Souvenir hunters often moved in behind the patrols and made off with what the Coast Guard had gathered.

The magazine complained that a great deal of valuable information on the ships and crew were lost in this way. For instance, it was known the *Richard H.* carried six life preservers. Several had been found on shore, and one was strapped to the body of a dead crewman. If the shore patrol knew for a certainly that scavengers had not taken off with one as a souvenir, they would know if there was the slightest chance of another crewman coming ashore in a life vest.

The wreckage from the *William B. Davock* littered the beach from Pentwater to south of Ludington where two of the ship's steel lifeboats were discovered Tuesday. Throughout the day, a total of sixteen bodies washed ashore with twelve identified as coming from the *Davock*. Two were identified as crewmen of the *Anna C. Minch*, and two remained unknown. One of the unidentified was found wearing a *Davock* life jacket, and the other body wore a life jacket with no markings. The life-jacketed bodies indicated the crews were either preparing to abandon ship or more likely had realized their ship was in grave danger of sinking and had prepared for the worst.

In Cleveland, Captain Thomas Zealand, marine superintendent of the Interlake Steamship Company, learned of the *Davock* sinking when an Associated Press reporter called to tell him bodies from his company's ship were washing ashore near Ludington. Zealand confirmed the sad news with a call to the Ludington Coast Guard station and rushed a three-man disaster team to the railroad station where they made connections to Ludington.

Word of the *Davock's* destruction rapidly spread by radio-telephone to many of the boats working the Great Lakes, that's how Captain Saunders of the *Jay C. Morse* learned of his son's death. One of the first bodies to be identified had been that of the James Saunders. The body of Saunders' young friend and fellow deckhand Sterling Woods stayed close even in death and was also quickly identified. The bodies of First Mate Charles Price, Second Mate Charles Wiesen, wheelmen Andy Stiffler and Walter Kiewice, and watchmen Lawrence Bleshoy and Martin Chambers also made a last landfall on Tuesday. Mrs. Lillian Bowman, who had called the home office to see if her husband would be home for Thanksgiving, learned that James would never make it home.

All of the bodies that found their way to shore on Tuesday and the next couple of days were from those of crewmen stationed at the bow of the *William B. Davock*. The first crewman from the aft end of the ship didn't make it to shore until the sixth day after it floundered. This supports the theory that the forward cabin and pilothouse were ripped off just prior to or as the ship plummeted to the bottom of the lake.

What didn't go down with the *Anna C. Minch* came ashore along six miles of beach near Pentwater. That at least some of the debris came from the *Minch* was confirmed by life preservers from the doomed ship. Four bodies were found among the wreckage near Pentwater. Another body recovered near Ludington plus those found at Pentwater all wore Canadian-type life preservers—pretty clear evidence the sailors came from the *Minch*. A badly damaged life boat from the *Minch* along with other wreckage including a compass and an outdated crew list in a metal tube made it conclusive.

The obvious escaped John O. McKellar, fleet superintendent of the Sarnia Steamships, Ltd. McKellar told the Associated Press he was convinced the *Minch* could survive any storm and then stepped back from his optimism a bit by offering the thought that maybe the ship had beached on one of the islands in the vicinity of Ludington. The fleet superintendent also denied that the bodies coming ashore were from the *Minch* in spite of the fact they wore *Minch* life jackets. Four of the Canadian crewman, George Sovey, James Becker, R. Elyea, and Lawrence Thompson, were positively identified by Tuesday evening.

Anxious wives, parents, and children in Milwaukee, Detroit, Toledo, Ashtabula, Toronto, and a dozen more cities and towns edging the Great Lakes spent a sleepless Tuesday night mourning the loss of a loved one, or, against all hope, prayed that their family member would beat the odds and somehow survive. Thousands more in towns from Duluth, Minnesota, in the west to Erie, Pennsylvania, in the east had a loved one or knew of someone aboard a vessel that was caught in the storm and spent many anxious hours awaiting word of their safety.

Chapter 14

"It Looked Like the Parting
of the Red Sea."

On Tuesday morning, Michigan lay in shambles. Power was out in many parts of the state, telephone service was either nonexistent or downed long-distance lines cut off communities from the outside world. Overturned trees and grounded power lines closed roads and highways, and the wind still shrieked like a banshee. The storm roiled the waters of the Detroit River to such an extent it released the body of a man who had been in the water for nearly a year. Police were investigating.

In Saginaw, Bay City, and Michigan's Thumb, the storm repeated the cyclonic histrionics it had visited on Chicago, Milwaukee, Ludington, Grand Rapids, and other towns in the Midwest. Trees, telephone poles, chimneys, power lines, roofs, and old buildings all suffered the same fate as those the storm had earlier encountered. At Bay City, however, the wind found something new to mess with.

The southwest to northeast axis of shallow Saginaw Bay was almost perfectly aligned with the direction of the storm making it all the easier for the wall of wind to empty the bay like somebody had pulled a drain plug. The water level in the Saginaw River and the bay dropped more than 9 feet on Monday night and Tuesday morning. Old wrecks and hulks that had spent a generation or more on the river bottom were resting high and, if not entirely dry, in plain view of the curious.

On the saucer-shallow bay, the shoreline, near the mouth of the Saginaw River, receded a good mile-and-a-half to the north. To the west, at Bay City State Park, the park superintendent said the bay was a good half-mile out from the usual shoreline. On the east side of Saginaw Bay where the water is hardly waist deep over a large area known as the "flats," it looked like the parting of the Red

Sea. Open water was barely visible several miles off shore and closer inshore fishing tugs sat in the mud. The area's commercial fishermen took the unique opportunity to walk out to nets that were usually under water and repair them in place. They also went walking in search of nets carried away in the storm.

The receding waters spawned a new type of fishing. As water was blown out of the bay, fish were trapped in shallow pools left between sandbars and small depressions or left to flop on the damp lake bottom. Locals grabbed pails and ventured out onto the nearly dry seabed and picked up fish by the bucket full. Instead of baiting a hook or netting their catch, the new fishermen sometimes landed their fish by chopping it out of frozen sand or scooping it from one of the shallow pools.

In addition to fish, the low or no water resulted in some industries in Bay City and along the Saginaw River sucking air. Water was a critical component in the manufacturing process for a number of Bay City factories. Most of these plants drew their own water from pipes that reached far out into the bay. When the pipes literally ran out of the water and temporarily rested above sea level, the factories had to shut down. Bay City also got its drinking water from the bay. Even though the intake pipe extended 3,800 feet off shore, it became fully exposed and the city had to rely on water held in the city reservoir until Saginaw Bay returned. That happened at 10:00 A.M. on Wednesday morning.

Farther north at the Straits of Mackinac, the ferry service linking Michigan's northern and lower peninsulas slowly and with great difficulty resumed operations. The Michigan Highway Department warned hunters of long back ups and that Mackinaw City and the whole Straits area was fast running out of food and groceries. On Wednesday, a line of cars parked bumper-to-bumper still stretched four miles south from the ferry docks, and this in spite of the fact that the ferry service set a hunting season record by carrying 8,824 hunters in 3,684 vehicles that day. When hunters finally reached the Upper Peninsula, they found many roads and trails into the woods still blocked by fallen trees.

On what had been a long Monday for Great Lake sailors and their ships, the freighter *Frank J. Peterson* received its share of bad luck when a lightning strike fried the steamer's navigational equipment. The freighter had been nearing the top end of Lake Michigan making for the Straits of Mackinac when the lightning bolt scored a direct hit. In confined waters with danger or disaster lurking at nearly every point of the compass, in close to zero visibility, and under assault by heavy seas, the ship somehow stayed out of trouble until early Tuesday morning when it struck St. Helena Island some ten miles west of the Straits. The *Peterson's* cargo included scrap iron, new automobiles, and general freight.

If the crew was eager to abandon ship, they were soon disappointed. In the coming week, a Coast Guard surfboat transported the ship's officers to St. Ignace where they bought groceries and supplies and then returned them to the grounded vessel. During the next few days, various attempts were made to pull the *Peterson* off the beach, and when they didn't work, a dredge tried to carve out a channel on which the freighter could be refloated. It was all to no avail. It was not until November 20 that the company ordered the ship abandoned and the crew taken off. The *Peterson* was to be left on the island for the winter.

After little deliberation and probably without wading through the multitude of tomes outlining maritime law pertaining to salvage operations, some locals decided to fly by the seat of their pants, legally speaking, and concluded the *Peterson* was an abandoned hulk ripe for salvage and treated the ship as if it was a "Big Lot" store. When the lake froze up, "salvagers" drove their cars and trucks across the ice and out to the ship and loaded straight from the cargo hold as if it was a "Customer Pickup Door." With the coming of spring in 1941, the *Peterson* was finally dragged off the beach. The ship was considerably lighter than when it ran aground.

⌐☗¬

In Green Bay, the *SS Sinaloa* and her forty-one-member crew had spent the night in the grip of the maelstrom. Soon after the *Sinaloa's* anchor line parted and sent her adrift, the ship's engine failed leaving her powerless. Driven before the storm throughout Monday night, the sand sucker finally went aground at 11:00 A.M. on Tuesday morning, 200 feet offshore in Big Bay De Noc's Sac

Bay on the Garden Peninsula. After the wild ride down Green Bay, the crew was surprised at how gently the big ship settled on a rocky ledge with her stern pointing toward the shore and higher than her partially submerged bow. She settled with a list to starboard which the captain corrected by ordering the port side sluices opened.

The grounded ship was pounded by waves that had the whole length of Green Bay in which to build up a head of steam, and if safety and dry land lay only 200 yards away, getting there from the *Sinaloa* looked about as doable as going over Niagara Falls in a barrel. The huge seas that beat against the sand sucker and roared ashore like an express train had grown even taller as the lake shoaled. Just before hitting the beach, the great, white-capped waves curled over and exploded in a fury of foam that had the power to pound a human body into something as pliable as a jellyfish. And if one somehow survived the 200 watery yards of mayhem and crawled up onto the sand edging Sac Bay, what then? The distant landscape looked as deserted and remote as Robinson Crusoe's island. Twenty-two crewmen were trapped in the aft section of the ship, the rest of the crew huddled together in the bow and wondered: What next?

If, as John G. Mitchell wrote in the November 1981 *Audubon Magazine*, the Upper Peninsula, "...still hangs on out there like a rawhide flap of the old frontier, out-posted from the swirl of mainstream America,"[34] the pre-Mackinac Bridge 1940 U.P. was even further removed from normal, everyday, pre-World War II America. The Garden Peninsula, then and now, was a world unto itself, peopled by sturdy, fearless, and ruggedly independent fishermen who called the place home. They were men of the sea and—it may well be encoded in the DNA of all who become a part of the brotherhood of the sea—they always went to the aid of their fellow sailors.

Waves were still sinking small fishing boats at their docks when news of the *Sinaloa's* stranding raced through the Garden Peninsula fishing villages of Fairport, Garden, and Fayette early Tuesday afternoon. Twenty-eight-year-old fisherman Cecil Shawl began bailing out his 14-foot rowboat while William Toles of Garden emptied out his 16-foot, flat-bottomed, pond net boat and began rowing south to the site of the grounding. Other fishermen from many points along the peninsula quickly followed suit and began making their way to the *Sinaloa*.

When Toles reached Sac Bay, he rowed through the breaking surf and heaved one end of a line to the *Sinaloa's* stern. The crew of the stranded ship quickly tied it off, and Toles headed to shore with the other end where it was hauled up a bluff and tied to a tree. The pond boat was then dragged hand-over-hand back to the *Sinaloa* and loaded with thirteen crewmen who were pulled ashore. On the second trip, the little boat pitched ten *Sinaloa* crewmen in the water when it capsized within yards of leaving the stranded ship. Miraculously, all ten managed to make it back aboard their ship while two fishermen, Cecil Shawl and Tom Peterson, rowed out to the capsized boat, righted it, and pulled it ashore.

On the third trip, both the rowboat and the pond boat, manned by Peterson and Shawl, made it to the beached ship where the sailors lined-up at the rail and, one at a time, slid down a rope and into one of the bobbing boats. Then came the perilous trip to shore in the still booming seas. Shawl got his boat safely to the beach by having the crewmen hang onto to the landline for dear life every time a big wave threatened to overturn the craft. The other boat rolled over in the crashing waves, but the desperate men reached for the landline and pulled themselves to safety. When the last of the waterlogged men struggled ashore, night had fallen and all of the twenty-two crewmen from the aft section of the *Sinaloa* had reached dry land.

Even as late as Tuesday evening, the waves crashing against the *Sinaloa* must have been of a size to wash across the straight deck and make it impossible for those in the bow to reach the stern where their fellow crewmen were being rescued. In the growing dark, two attempts were made to get a line to the bow section of the sand sucker, and both efforts resulted in the small rescue boat getting tossed ass over apple cart and catapulting the rescuers into the bay's still violent waters. Seeing the two failures and the danger inherent in any further attempts, the crew in the bow began flashing Morse Code with weak flashlights. This presented a problem for those on shore, because none of them knew Morse Code. Someone had the bright idea of sending for Soo Line Railroad agent D.J. O'Brien from Nahma Junction. He arrived on the scene with a big flashlight and began a lengthy discussion with the stranded crew via blinking flashlights. At 9:30 P.M. the Garden Peninsula fishermen told the crew trapped on the *Sinaloa's* bow they would begin rescue attempts again at dawn.

The wet and miserable survivors from the stern of the ship and their rescuers warmed themselves briefly at bonfires along the beach and then were taken fifteen miles north to the tiny village of Garden where Ed Purtill's bar had been turned into an impromptu first aid station and rescue headquarters. The men got out of their wet clothes and hung them up to dry, and chances are pretty good everyone had a stiff dose of the bar's emergency medicinal restorer. Garden's Justice of the Peace, Stanley Jacques took charge of first aid and attended to cuts and bruises. Most of the crew was suffering from some degree of exposure, and Jacques triaged the sailors, called ambulances, and sent three of the group to Escanaba's St. Francis Hospital. At least one of the rescued sailors reached Purtill's with a roll of sopping-wet greenbacks which proved perfectly acceptable to area merchants. One Escanaba clothier took shoes and socks to the survivors in Garden.

Meanwhile, a detail from the U.S. Coast Guard Station in Munising, on the U.P.'s Superior shore, was racing across the peninsula with a beach cart and breeches buoy. They arrived on the beach opposite the *Sinaloa* just before midnight on Tuesday and set to work with a sense of urgency, fearing the ship might slip off the reef and sink in deeper water with the crew still on board. The Coast Guard working party quickly set up lights so they could work at night and fired a line to the bow of the *Sinaloa* with a Lyle gun. After the line was made fast on shore and ship, a breeches buoy was hung from the line, pulled to the ship, and began taking off sailors.

For the nineteen crewmen on the bow, the trip ashore often meant one more miserable encounter with the icy, storm-tossed water. The landline sagged under the weight of the passenger and as the line stretched and the sag increased, the man in the canvas seat stood an excellent chance of being dunked like a tea bag in Lake Michigan. The second-to-last man off the wreck was Captain William C. Fontaine. The skipper was totally exhausted from exposure, stress, and 48 hours without sleep as he struggled to save his crew and ship. There was also cause for concern because Fontaine weighed nearly 300 pounds, making the breeches buoy a tight fit. His rescuers also knew his weight would make the landline sag even further during his transit. The first mate helped his captain into the canvas pants, checked to make sure all straps were secured and gave the signal to the men ashore to heave-ho. Fontaine was dunked early and often, and halfway to shore the breeches buoy and the captain completely disappeared under the waves. Those on the beach pulled madly on the line while others waded out into the surf to manhandle Fontaine ashore. The officer emerged from the surf more dead than alive. Rescuers rubbed him down to restore circulation and gave him a stimulant to bring him around. First Mate Harmon Burch of Grand Rapids, Michigan, followed the captain and was pulled to shore without incident, the last man off the ship.

Once on shore and with a stiff drink under his belt, a somewhat revived Captain Fontaine asked about the safety of his crew and then wanted to know who had gone out in a small boat to rescue sailors from the aft section of the *Sinaloa*. "I'm one of the suckers,"[35] replied Tom Peterson. Fontaine expressed his appreciation and said, "Every one who went out ought to have medals."[36]

The captain and the men who came off the ship with him were rushed to Garden and the bar/rescue headquarters where they received first-aid for contusions, bumps, and bruises, and it was determined that, like their fellow crewmen from the stern, they also suffered from exposure. Seven more of the crew were sent to the hospital in Escanaba making a total of eleven men from the *Sinaloa* who were hospitalized as a result of their wild night at sea and dangerous rescue.

Chapter 15

"One of the Most Unheralded & Amazing Air-rescue Feats in Civil Aviation History."

As a counterpoint to the Valkyrie wail of the wind across the Mississippi wetlands during the darkness of Monday night and early Tuesday morning came faintly heard calls for help and the occasional discharge of a shotgun. Death was stalking the hunters on the open pools, marshes, mudflats, and reedy sandbars bordering the Mississippi, and joining the audible calls for help were numberless silent or whispered prayers.

All available deputy sheriffs, conservation officers, and rescue squads had been in the field since Monday evening. By Tuesday morning, every marina and landing on the Mississippi from the Twin Cities in the north to Prairie du Chien in the south was packed with cars full of hunters' families, friends, and loved ones who sat and waited for word of the missing.

Rescue central for the Winona area was the Minnesota city's boat launching site. The sheriff, county coroner, and police commissioner were all on hand along with game wardens and national wildlife refuge rangers. The various officers organized upwards of a hundred volunteers into groups that began a systematic search of the vast wetlands. Rescuers were joined by the curious and families and friends of duck hunters who were still missing. Both the living and dead found by the different rescue groups working in and around the Winona area were funneled back through the city's landing site on the Mississippi. The city garage in Winona was converted to a temporary morgue where the frozen bodies were left to thaw and be identified.

Rescuers were heartened Tuesday morning when the wind seemed to moderate slightly, but less wind gentled the turbulent water and allowed ice to form more rapidly. The quickly spreading

Snow and ice cover the Mississippi wetlands in the
immediate aftermath of the Armistice Day Storm.

Photo courtesy of the Winona County Historical Society.

ice became a major obstacle to survival and rescue because it nearly
always proved to be too thick to row or paddle through and too thin
to walk on. Wading in freezing water was misery enough without
breaking through ice with every step. And then there were the ice
pile-ups. The wind drove the ice onto the land were it piled up on
shore to such a height and depth hunters couldn't push their boats
over or through the build up. The ice even made it difficult to drag
for bodies where it was suspected boats had capsized and hunters
might have drowned.

Ice became much less of a problem for rescuers when the
Army Corps of Engineers' diesel tug, the *Joseph Thockmorton* and the
launch *Chippewa* were assigned as rescue craft on the Mississippi
north of Winona. They were soon joined by the U.S. Coast Guard
vessel *Wake Robin*.

The rescue squads and boats working the vast wetlands saved
countless lives and encountered enough tragedy to last a lifetime. A

rescue party near St. Paul stumbled across and followed the trail of three duck hunters who had been reported lost on Tuesday morning. Rescuers struck the hunters' trail at their overturned boat and followed their tracks to the remains of a small fire on a nearby island. The trail then led from hope to despair as the searchers tracked the trio from the cold fire to a large hole in the ice. The rescue party believed the ice gave way under the weight of the three men and hope for their survival evaporated.

The positions of the bodies of two hunters from Eau Claire, Wisconsin, told rescuers of the pair's desperate quest for shelter. Their boat apparently went down while trying to reach a railroad embankment that marked the edge of a large pool. Both men made it to shore through the icy water and started up the steep incline to the railroad bed. If they could reach the top, the tracks would point to safety. Rescuers found the first hunter's body hanging on to a tree a few steps from the waterline. Farther up the slope death overtook his companion as he was in the act of reaching for his next handhold.

Many of the dead brought into Winona and other river towns bore deep bruises where they had pounded and beat themselves or their friends in a desperate attempt to stay warm and keep the blood circulating. One man was found standing upright in shallow water with one frozen hand grasping an overhead branch. The rescue team found it easiest to cut the branch on either side of the death grip and transported the deceased to the morgue still clutching the limb.

From a hospital bed in Winona, 17-year-old Gerald Tarras recalled watching family members and his friend Bill die on Monday night and Tuesday. In prose that is almost Hemingway-esque, he told a reporter from the *Winona Republican-Herald*, "We went out about ten in the morning, the four of us. It was warm and raining. The wind came at noon. We began to worry. My dad said we'd better go back. It got fierce. Then Bill Wernecke died. He was cold. We boxed each other to keep warm. Bill died. I was holding him. He went, 'O-h-h-h…,' and he was gone.

"We were standing in water. We had a black Labrador dog with us. My brother died next. Yes, he died. I knew he was dead. He was cold. An airplane flew over and I moved my arm. It saw us.

Then my dad died. They took me off in a government tug and gave me some coffee."[37]

Gerald lost his friend, Bill Wernecke, around 2:00 A.M. on Tuesday morning, his brother died at 11:00 A.M., and his father hung on another three hours before he passed away at 2:00 P.M. Less than an hour later, rescuers reached Gerald, who was sitting on a stump holding his dog. The Lab probably saved his master's life, and it wasn't the only instance that night of a dog's body heat making the difference between life and death. Gerald also owed his life to Max Conrad, the pilot who had spotted him from the air and directed rescuers to his location.

Dawn had barely creased the sky on Tuesday morning when Max got a telephone call asking if he could get a plane aloft in the near impossible flying conditions and search for lost hunters in the backwaters of the Mississippi. Winds were still blowing in excess of 50 mph, and a man could hardly stand up in the gusts, but Max said he'd give it a try. Conrad called several friends and some of his students and asked them to meet him at his little flying school bordering a farm-field runway.

A Piper Cub sat just inside the hanger, and if it wasn't going to be used, it would have to be moved to get to other planes. Max decided he might as well take the Piper Cub and climbed into the cockpit and started the engine. His makeshift ground crew composed of friends and students opened the hangar doors and dragged the little plane tail-first out into a wind that was roaring across the airfield at highway speeds. It took five people on each wing to hold the plane to the earth until it was pointed into the wind. Conrad fed the engine some throttle, the ground crew let go, and the plane took off—backwards. Once in the air, Max found that, at best, the plane could make about 20 mph flying into the wind, regardless of the fact the airspeed indicator registered 80 mph. When he headed the plane down wind, he estimated the Piper Cub sped across the landscape at 120 mph.

Within minutes of lifting into the storm-tossed sky, Conrad flew over a vast pool edging the great river and spotted the first of many hunters who would owe their lives to him. That first pool revealed a young man frozen up to his waist in ice while his dog ran along the edge of the slough. The lad waved at the plane then keeled over on the ice. On a second pass, Conrad spotted a boat under the ice and what looked like two bodies next to it. In the willows near the shore, the pilot spotted another man hanging onto the lower branches of a willow tree. He thought the man might still be alive.

Stunned by the life-and-death struggle going on below him, Conrad was sorely tempted to try and land near the tragic scene and render immediate assistance. He knew landing here would almost certainly result in wrecking the plane, so he reluctantly turned back to the airfield to report his findings and hope rescuers could reach the party in time to save the two lives.

Landing at the airfield had its own challenges. The Piper Cub's landing speed equaled the speed of the wind blowing across the airfield. In landing, he would be virtually standing still. If that wasn't difficult enough, once he touched down and throttled back the engine, the wind might very well flip the light plane on its back. As he came within inches of touch down, his ad hoc ground crew grabbed the Piper Cub and muscled it into the hangar. Conrad jumped from the plane, picked up a phone, and reported his findings to the local authorities. After a brief rest and some hurried instructions, Conrad climbed back in the Piper Cub, was dragged out of the hangar by his ground crew, and once again launched backwards into one of the most unheralded and amazing air-rescue feats in civil aviation history.

To repeatedly take off and land in these extreme flying conditions might be courting disaster, yet that is what Conrad did for the rest of the day. He was sometimes accompanied by a spotter, and after the first flight, he carried along five gallon cans packed with sandwiches, whiskey, cigarettes, and matches that he dropped to stranded hunters. On locating a party or a single survivor, he would make a pass over the spot, turn off his engine, open the cockpit door, and shout encouragement, telling those below help was on the way and drop his care package in a can. He often used the Piper Cub as a guide dog and led the lost through channels and waterways to safety. On finding an overturned boat, Conrad would take his little single-engine plane so low it was skimming across sandbars and marsh grass as he tried peering under the boat looking for survivors.

On his third flight of the day, which would have been about 11:00 A.M., Max discovered three men frozen stomach deep in ice. On his first flyby, only one moved. He banked the aircraft and headed off searching for a rescue party. Finding one, he returned to the three hunters and circled them until help arrived. Miraculously, all three survived.

When the Army Corp of Engineers' boats made it to the Winona area, Conrad would often circle above stranded hunters until one of the boats arrived. If he spotted hunters that were fairly distant from a rescue craft, he would start the men in the direction of the boat and then fly to the boat and get it headed toward the stranded men. Conrad became so efficient in locating lost hunters and pointing the lost and the rescuers on convergent courses, the rescue boats wasted little time in aimless searching.

Harold Easeman of Winona was a typical recipient of Conrad's heroics. Easeman was hunting with two friends when the storm caught them on a bog. They were rowing furiously in a desperate bid to reach shelter when an oarlock on their boat broke. The trio overturned the boat making it into a windbreak, managed to get a fire started, and hung on through the night. In the morning, they heard a plane and fired their shotguns but failed to attract the pilot's attention. Hope sprang anew a couple hours later when, again, they heard the plane overhead and this time were spotted.

Easeman told the *Milwaukee Journal*, "Conrad yelled down at us from the open door of the plane, 'Sit tight, we will get you out of here.' In a few minutes he was back with a tin of food and cigarettes and dropped it. He kept flying over us, then hollered down: 'Start out and go in the direction I am.'

"We took our shotguns and started. Conrad shouted, 'Leave your guns and take the skiff.' We did. We broke through ice several times, then we would hang onto the skiff and work it along to new ice. The tug *Throckmorton* picked us up. Conrad saved our lives."[38]

Conrad flew from about 9:00 in the morning until it was too dark to see and risked his life more in one day than a matador does in a lifetime. On Wednesday morning, Conrad was back in the air looking for more survivors.

Two rescues that took place in Wisconsin on Tuesday could have used the likes of Max Conrad. In a thirteen-hour ordeal of grit and determination, Columbia County Sheriff Harry Hibner and a rescue posse of six battled the deadly wind, cold, and snow to reach a party of eight duck hunters stranded on an island in the Wisconsin River north of Madison. The hunters, trapped for 22 hours, suffered from exposure and exhaustion.

It took eight hours of work to rescue four duck hunters from a cabinless island three-quarters-of-a-mile offshore in Lake Winnebago in eastern Wisconsin. The four had rented blinds on Long Point Island and spent the night in the open. A rescue party, composed of sheriff deputies and conservation officers, tried twice to reach the island with power boats but was turned back by high waves. Finally, the sheriff and his deputies floated out to the island on a barge that was tethered to the shore by a long rope. They loaded up the hunters and were pulled back to the mainland by a county highway truck. The four hunters, suffering from mild exposure, were taken to Oshkosh Hospital.

Chapter 16

"Spam Fans Were as Ubiquitous as Snowflakes."

While much of the Midwest inched toward normalcy on Tuesday, Minnesota remained locked in the blizzard's grip. In Chicago and Milwaukee, Tuesday was a day for clean up. Telephone and utility companies worked overtime to restore power and phone service while road crews removed downed trees, poles, and the debris from wind-wracked buildings. In the Windy City, life was pretty much back to normal by Tuesday night with Milwaukee not much further behind. Obviously, it was an entirely different world along the Mississippi where the frantic search for survivors continued throughout the day and much of the night. Nothing was back to even near normal by Tuesday night in Minnesota.

When the citizen's of Minneapolis and St. Paul woke on Tuesday and tried to leave their homes or apartments, they discovered their twin communities were buried in snow and trapped in an icy gridlock. Virtually every residential street in both cities was choked with snowdrifts and countless buried and abandoned cars. Joining the mess on every major thoroughfare were stalled trucks and derailed or hopelessly snowbound streetcars. The streets couldn't be plowed because of all the abandoned vehicles, and the abandoned vehicles couldn't be moved because of the snow. Due to the clogged streets, at least one home in the greater Twin Cities area burned to the foundation because fire trucks couldn't make their way to the fire.

The thousands of office workers who spent Monday night filling all of Minneapolis' hotel rooms and overflowing into hallways, lobbies, and dining rooms woke up hungry on Tuesday. Downtown restaurants and grocery stores were pressed to the limits to feed the host. It slowly dawned on those who spent Monday night downtown that, as the day wore on, chances weren't improving they would get home today either. By nightfall, most of those who couldn't get home Monday found themselves spending another night in the city center.

Warner's Hardware in Minneapolis was either demonstratively better at predicting the weather than the U.S. Weather Bureau or the store had made a special arrangement with the newspaper to run a specific ad after a snow storm. In the November 12 Minneapolis Morning Tribune, a Warner's ad offered snow shovels on sale for 69 cents.

At farmhouses and lonely country homes across the state, Minnesotans woke up Tuesday and found the storm had literally imprisoned them. On opening the front door, many residents found they were facing a solid mass of snow that the wind had piled and then packed into their home's doorway. People crawled out windows on the side of the house with the shallowest drifts, schlepped through the snow, fetched a shovel, and started digging out the doorway. When that was done, many farmers had to dig a path to the barn and/or the outdoor convenience.

As it had on Monday, the storm created small, impromptu, and wholly original communities that had the life span of a fruit fly, wherever snowdrifts and accidents forced travelers to find temporary shelter in out-of-the-way places. Bernice Elwell was returning to North Dakota from Minneapolis when the storm struck. She and her four traveling companions were only ten miles from St. Cloud when they found the road blocked by giant drifts. Elwell and her friends pulled into a lonely, four-room farmhouse and asked for shelter. The house lay near the point where the road became impassable, and by dawn on Tuesday it was jammed with 200 travelers seeking refuge from the storm.

The farm family killed all their chickens and made pancakes in an attempt to feed the crowd. A coffee salesman shared all the candy bars he happened to have, and a truck driver handed out fruit. The house didn't have an indoor toilet, and many in the crowd either didn't like the idea of using an outhouse or didn't want to brave the elements, so instead they adjourned to an upstairs bedroom where they used jars and every other container they could turn into an instant chamber pot. It quickly turned into a mess.

Smokers who ran out of cigarettes began purchasing them at 50 cents apiece from a man who had several cartons. After a few not-so-veiled threats about price gouging, the cost fell to a still exorbitant 15 cents a butt, and those suffering from nicotine withdrawal made no further complaints. It was not until the afternoon of the twelfth that the road to St. Cloud opened and the travelers began to depart. One can only wonder what the house looked like by late Tuesday afternoon.

One of Minnesota's and the storm's worst traffic jams and largest congregations of stranded motorists occurred in New Brighton just a few miles north of St. Paul. Today, the town lies within the beltway circling the Twin Cities. The traffic deadlock began when a car stalled in the intersection of County Road D and Highway 8. A second stalled auto joined the first, and the *coup de grâce* was administered by a loaded passenger bus that plowed into the second car. The intersection and both roads were now plugged like a cork in a bottle, and traffic started backing up in all directions. It was bumper cars in an amusement park as autos piled into each other and became hopelessly entangled. The line of stalled and wrecked vehicles made a perfect snow fence, and soon the entire traffic jam was buried in growing snowdrifts.

Dozens of stranded travelers were shuttled to the town hall by wreckers and other emergency vehicles, and it was soon jammed with an overflow crowd. Early in the evening, the first hand was dealt in what would turn out to be an all night bridge game that was closely followed by a densely packed circle of kibitzers. Another group started a sing-a-long that was soon joined by most of the crowd. The town marshal served sandwiches throughout the night, and Milton Steger brewed and served forty-five gallons of coffee, which may account for the fact that most of those in the town hall got no sleep that night. Another equally good reason for the group insomnia is that everyone was having too good a time.

A tavern sitting on one corner of the intersection, at the very epicenter of the traffic jam held another fifty marooned motorists. The tavern keeper worked the night making coffee and sandwiches, and those who found sleep at the tavern did so in chairs or sprawled out on beer cases, kegs, the bar, and odd corners of the floor. A relief

Stuck and abandoned cars near the Twin Cities.
Photo courtesy of the Minnesota Historical Society.

column of snowplows fought their way through the huge drifts and opened the way to Minneapolis late on Tuesday, but motorists were warned wind and snow could and probably would re-close the road soon. Hundreds emptied out of New Brighton, but for the bus passengers and those whose cars were entangled with other autos and still entombed in snow, it meant a second night in the little town.

As late as Tuesday night, over fifty cars and trucks and better than a 100 travelers remained stranded in the small village of Vernon Center in south central Minnesota. Locals had opened their homes, and some residents took in as many as eight strangers. The village's meat market quickly sold out, and with no bread or grocery trucks moving and farmers unable to get their dairy products to town, a food shortage seemed a real possibility. The road to Mankato was finally opened late Tuesday night.

Many motorists found themselves trapped on lonely stretches of road far removed from the safety offered by small towns or remote farms. When a honeymooning couple from Canada found themselves driving in Monday's whiteout, they stopped the car hoping visibility would improve only to become snowbound, marooned, and unable to see more than a few feet in any direction. It is unclear whether they were on their way to or returning from Florida, or in the first blush of marriage simply believed they had their love to keep them warm because the newlyweds were neither wearing winter clothes nor had they packed any.

When freezing to death seemed likely, the couple abandoned the car and struck off into the whiteout looking for help. In what was a life and death gamble with long, longs odds against survival, the couple came up winners. The honeymooners hadn't gone far when they literally ran into a wall, which they followed until they encountered a door. The couple had stumbled across a stout little shed filled with sheep. The animals warmed the place enough to keep the newlyweds from freezing to death until they were found by a farmer late Tuesday when he showed up to check on his livestock. In a honeymoon to remember, the woman was taken to a hospital and treated for frostbite.

In similar circumstances, another group of travelers decided the best chance for survival lay with staying in the snowbound car. The car's five passengers and driver found themselves miles from help but with a nearly full gas tank. With no possible refuge or shelter in sight, they decided it would be foolish to set off on foot. Instead, they agreed to run the car for fifteen minutes out of every hour in order to keep the temperature in the car above freezing. The night passed and the sky lightened into a sunless, monochromatic grey. Time slowly ticked by with no help on the horizon and the gas gage inching toward empty. After 30 hours of imprisonment, a snowplow finally freed the party at 5:00 P.M. on Tuesday.

Late Tuesday night after 24 hours of attacking snowdrifts and dragging stuck and stalled cars off roads and out of ditches and plowing the roadways, the Minnesota Highway Department announced they had opened less than 10% of the state's main highways. Motorists were warned it was still unsafe to travel.

Hell may have descended on Winona, Minnesota, Monday and Tuesday, but it didn't prove powerful enough to keep a Spam advertising campaign off the streets and out of the newspaper. As reported by the Spam Man, yes the Spam Man, in an ad disguised as an article in the Winona Herald-Republican on November 13, 1940, under the headline "Blizzard Has No Effect On Spam $ Bill Payment," the Spam Man and Spam Girl, each armed with $2 bills, mushed through the streets of Winona and neighboring small towns on the hunt for Spam eaters and their testimonials.

When found, the lovers of the meat-that-comes-in-a-can had to verify and affirm their culinary predilection by producing the key and the metal strip said key peeled from the can during the mouth-watering ritual of liberating the mystery meat from its tin cocoon.

Thus, while workers struggled to open roads, restore power and telephone service, and rescuers desperately searched for marooned duck hunters or retrieved their bodies, Spam Man and Spam Girl wandered through a river town gripped by tragedy and buffeted by one of the worst storms in recorded history on the lookout for Spam lovers, specifically, those consumers who had the presence of mind Tuesday morning to include the key and metal strip off an opened can of processed meat among their essential survival gear before venturing out of the house.

According to Spam Man, Spam fans were as ubiquitous as snowflakes that day. Amid the kudos paid by fanciers of the meat that comes shaped like a paving stone was a man who claimed he liked it, "...just as it comes from the can."[39] And without a hint of sarcasm or a moment's consideration for the events unfolding around her, an Alma, Minnesota, woman said, "Spam is tasty, economical, quick to serve, and can be kept on hand for emergencies."[40]

In a clear case of overstating the obvious, Spam Man closed the article by saying, "We will contact you when you least expect it."[41]

WEDNESDAY
&
THURSDAY

Chapter 17

"Their Calmness Averted
Any Threat of Panic."

The mournful search for debris and bodies from the two lost fishing tugs continued throughout Wednesday with U.S. Coast Guardsmen from Benton Harbor to Muskegon searching the waters of Lake Michigan and walking the shoreline in the vicinity of South Haven. The name plate from the *Richard H.* was discovered resting on the sand at Grand Haven State Park, and a life jacket also from the fishing tug turned up. Especially disturbing was the broken straps on the life jacket, which probably meant the preserver had been worn by a crew member when he went into the water. The sheer violence of the storm had, either before or after death, ripped the life jacket from his body. More small pieces of flotsam from the fishing tugs reached shore that day but no bodies.

Thursday, the people of South Haven kept one ear cocked for the sound of the city's power plant whistle that would signal the start of a community-wide celebration. The South Haven Coast Guard surfboat and her crew were due to return home, and the city planned on a grand reception for the local heroes. Finally at 4:45 P.M., the whistle blew and it was soon joined by car horns and church bells as the surfboat was spotted nearing port. Townspeople by the hundreds raced to the Coast Guard Station on the south pier and by 5:15 P.M., when the surfboat touched the dock, the crowd had grown to an estimated 1,500 celebrants. Boatswain's Mate Dudley, in charge of the surfboat, was first off. He waded through the throng of well-wishers and greeted other guardsmen with a smile and said, "We had a swell trip, boys. That's one you missed."[42]

Finally, at 9:30 A.M. on Saturday, a half-mile south of the Grand Haven breakwater, a body from the *Richard H.* came ashore. The deceased was fully clothed, wore a life jacket, and was initially

Crew of the South Haven USCG powered surf boat returning to South Haven.
Photo courtesy of the Michigan Maritime Museum.

miss-identified as Stanley White until someone who knew John Taylor Jr., a machinist and engineer on the *Richard H.*, positively identified his body. John's three brothers arrived late Saturday and confirmed the identity.

It was discovered that John had gone into the water wearing a wristwatch that had stopped at 2:53. The Taylor brothers told officials that John faithfully wound the watch every morning and it would have stopped within six minutes of being immersed in the water. All of which seemed to indicate the *Richard H.* went to the bottom in mid-afternoon less than two hours after a horrific squall tore through the area.

Taylor's body was taken to Rhinelander, Wisconsin, for burial. The Great Lakes fisherman was 36 when the *Richard H.* made its last voyage; he had been a crewman for the past two years and it was the only boat on which he had ever worked. John left a wife and two sons, seven and nine years old. His was the only body from either of the South Haven fishing tugs that Lake Michigan ever gave up.

T

At 8:30 A.M. Wednesday morning, a power surfboat was launched at Ludington and headed for the grounded *City of Flint* where it took soundings and returned at 1:00 P.M. to take off the ferry's four passengers. It had been a most unusual adventure for the quartet who had boarded the ship in Wisconsin for what would have normally been a few hours' voyage. Instead, they were treated to a carnival ride through one of the worst storms to ever hit the Great Lakes, a near shipwreck, and being stranded for nearly 24 hours aboard a grounded ship. Through it all, the four had been greatly impressed with the spirit and professionalism of the *City of Flint's* crew. To pay them their due, the passengers composed, signed, and sent the following statement to the *Ludington Daily News.* "We, passengers aboard the *City of Flint* when it was beached off Ludington November 11, wish to express our appreciation of the manner in which the crew conducted themselves during the entire period of the emergency.

"Their calmness averted any threat of panic, and their friendly co-operation while the ship was beached kept up our morale and spirits.

"We feel that it was only the able seamanship of the captain and crew on watch at the time we struck that averted complete disaster."[43]

The crew and Coast Guard dismantled the breeches buoy apparatus, and it was returned to the station on Wednesday. The wrecking tug *Cushing* arrived from Chicago in the afternoon and attached lines to the beached ferry and began trying to drag it off the shoaling lake bed and into deeper water. Freeing the big ship proved to be no easy task.

Car Ferry 21 also attached a line to its sister ship and joined the tug in working through the night. Searchlights from both the *Cushing* and *Car Ferry 21* caught the stranded ship in their mega-watt crosshairs and illuminated the scene like it was the center ring of a three-ring circus. The operation drew spectators to the beach by the hundreds for the free show that ran into Thursday with cars lining Lakeshore Drive. The *City of Flint* was inched northward by the *Cushing* and *Car Ferry 21* until the pride of the fleet broke free of the lake bed and once again rode the waves. After a brief inspection to check her seaworthiness, the *Cushing* towed the *City of Flint* to a dry dock in Manitowoc, Wisconsin, where the car ferry was subjected to a rigorous examination that found it had sustained surprisingly little damage. Two-thousand tons of ice was chipped off and steamed away, and fifteen bottom plates were replaced. Workers removed a lot of sand that had worked into the hull and refitted the ship with a new starboard propeller, a rudder, and stern post. The *City of Flint* was back in service in two weeks.

⚓

The three-man disaster response team from Cleveland's Interlake Steamship Company arrived in Ludington early Wednesday morning. The first stop for Ray Meyer, William Eckert, and George Manthey was the Dorrell Funeral Home where they made arrangements for the bodies coming from the *William B. Davock.* Small town funeral homes like those in Ludington were simply not prepared to meet the volume of dead that confronted them. So although all the bodies were taken to the Dorrell Funeral Home, morticians from the town's two other funeral homes joined with Dorrell to identify the bodies and prepare them for shipment home.

The team from Cleveland then made the sad walk to the Salvation Army Home that had been set up as an emergency morgue. Eleven men from the *William B. Davock* had made it to the morgue before the disaster response team arrived, and the trio began to double-check the identities of the eight bodies previously identified. They compared each body against a company document bearing the crew's names along with physical descriptions that included distinguishing scars, tattoos, and other peculiarities. Meyer and his team then moved on to the three yet unidentified bodies and found wheelman Andy Stiffler.

Cooperation turned to a cold shoulder when Meyer contacted the Ludington Coast Guard Station with some questions. Chief Boatswain Kristofferson, commander of the station, told Meyer he didn't have time for questions, and when the Interlake representative asked if he could speak with a Coast Guard crew member who might be able to answer his questions, the chief boatswain told Meyer the man had more important things to do. Kristofferson later even refused to take a phone call from Mr. Meyer.

In the afternoon, Manthey, Eckert, and Meyer began walking the beaches between Pentwater and Ludington on the lookout for more bodies and wreckage that might hint at the demise of the *Davock*. The team found much of the shoreline strewn with debris from the ship, some of it so pulverized as to be unidentifiable. They also came across two lifeboats from the *Davock* that had been washed ashore.

Meyer had visited with Captain Allen on the *William B. Davock* only a few weeks prior to the tragedy and remembered seeing a large wicker chair in the captain's office. The chair was clearly wider than the door, and the captain admitted it took some work to squeeze the thing through the narrow entryway. North of Ludington, Meyer found Captain Allen's wicker chair delivered whole onto the beach. The chair was convincing evidence that the forward cabins had been torn from the *Davock* just before or in the final act of going down. Also supporting the wicker chair evidence was the fact that, to date, all eleven of the bodies that had come ashore were men stationed in the forward section of the ship. Lawrence Gonyea, who worked in the stern didn't arrive on the beach until November 17, and fireman Frank Parker's body didn't wash ashore until the thirtieth. Another body was discovered on the sand December 18. Even though the sailor wore a gold signet ring engraved with the letters "T.F." and "From Mother," inside the gold band, the body couldn't be identified. Later in December, yet another *William B. Davock* crewman was found, and again the body defied repeated attempts to pin a name to it.

⚓

Captain Scott Misener, president of Sarnia Steamships Ltd., also stepped off a train in Ludington early Wednesday and went about the task of identifying and taking charge of any bodies from the *Anna C. Minch*. All efforts to discover the identity of a young man known only as a crewman of the *Minch* failed, and Misener made arrangement for the body to be shipped to Toronto. By late morning, he could be found walking the Lake Michigan shoreline in search of crew members and wreckage. Inevitably, he was drawn to the site where a wooden lifeboat bearing the name of the *Minch* was found eight miles south of Ludington. Grain from the sunken freighter was found washed up on the beach from Ludington to Pentwater. Surprisingly, some was in good enough condition that beachcombers carted away what they thought was still edible. Hikers on Sunday came across an unlikely sight at the point where Bass Lake empties into Lake Michigan. So much grain had come ashore at that spot it had clogged the outlet and dammed Bass Lake.

Chapter 18

The Fisherman Refused the Offered Bankroll and Told Steip, "Hell No, Captain. Glad to be of Service."

As dawn creased the sky on Wednesday, the situation on board the *Novadoc* had ratcheted up past desperate. The crew in the forward section of the ship had been without food and hardly any heat for nearly 36 hours. The men in the aft section of the broken and beached ship were in even worse straits. That morning, Captain Steip had made a notation in the ship's log that he didn't expect all the crew could make it through another day, and that was written before the captain had examined any of the crew trapped in the ship's stern section. He knew that anyone back there had to be in pretty bad shape after spending two days in the partially submerged cabin. Peterson, the most severely injured crewman in the stern cabin had been lying in freezing water for better than 24 hours. Conditions had gotten so desperate that, even with all his injuries, Peterson along with several other men in the stern resolved to try and swim to shore if help didn't arrive by the end of the day.

If there was any reason for optimism, it was that during the night the seas had abated and were no longer crashing over the hulk. The men in the captain's quarters knew someone was alive in the stern section because they had seen someone tossing water out of a porthole, but who and how many? As soon as it was light enough to see, Captain Steip carefully set off for the aft cabins over the ice-coated open deck.

When Steip stepped through the door into the partially flooded aft cabin, he learned both cooks had perished, and he could plainly see Peterson was in very poor condition and suffering from multiple wounds and exposure. As for the wounded fireman, when Steip entered the cabin it was the first Peterson knew for sure that anyone in the bow had survived the wreck. The captain quickly decided the men would be better off forward with the rest of the crew. They wouldn't have to stand in icy water and would benefit from even the miniscule amount of heat generated by the smoldering fire in the pail. Peterson told his shipmates to leave him because he knew he couldn't make the journey over a deck laminated in ice. The crew refused to abandon the substitute fireman, and several bent to the task of carrying him forward. Peterson's mates made steady progress with the injured seaman until they came to the great gash in the deck where the ship had broken in two. At 265 pounds, Peterson was just too heavy to lift across, so they lowered him to the deck, and he somehow managed to get on all fours and, as he later recalled, hopped the break, "like a frog."[44] The *Novadoc's* surviving crew members were soon reunited in the cabin's office.

The weather had begun to moderate shortly after midnight on Wednesday morning, and by daylight, there were many area sailors who had run out of patience waiting for the Coast Guard to mount a rescue. Strangely enough, the Pentwater Coast Guard Station and the men under Chief Boatswain Anderson had been told that very morning to exercise restraint and patience in reaching the *Novadoc*. Chief Boatswain Kristofferson, the area commander, had called the Pentwater Station at 6:00 A.M. and told his men not to be in a rush to reach the ship. They were to let the weather ease off even more and make sure everything was in readiness for a rescue attempt. Kristofferson's view was that a couple of more hours wouldn't mean life or death to those on the wreck.

Totally fed up with the efforts or lack thereof from the U.S. Coast Guard and unable to get the shipwrecked crew off his mind, Clyde Cross had been up all night. The veteran fisherman later testified that he felt the Coast Guard's motor lifeboat could have and should have been launched from Ludington shortly after midnight and gone to the *Novadoc's* aid. It also angered him that the Coast Guard did not even have one boat in the water at Pentwater that was prepared to render assistance. The veteran Great Lakes sailor also believed the equipment on the beach cart could have been lugged piecemeal to Jupiter Beach, and the crew might have been brought off by breeches buoy on Tuesday.

After hours of watching time slowly unwind Tuesday night and into Wednesday morning without any sign of activity from the Coast Guard, Cross finally reached his tipping point. He collected his crew and made for the *Three Brothers II*. They would rescue the crew of the *Novadoc*. Later, when asked under oath why he went out and brought off the stranded crew, Cross replied, "I figured they [the Coast Guard] could have been out a little sooner. I figured I could help them some. When they [the Coast Guard] turned down my boat I went out myself."[45]

As Clyde Cross and his crew prepared to set out from Pentwater, the local Coast Guard contingent, under Chief Boatswain Anderson, bestirred itself and launched a rescue attempt that turned into a pratfall. No, make that two pratfalls. One Coast Guard motorized surfboat had been in the water for at least a few hours on Wednesday morning, but when the crew tumbled aboard, they found the engine wouldn't start and there was neither a qualified mechanic at the post to make repairs nor any member of the crew who felt they were even competent to tinker with the engine. So it sat useless at the dock.

All was not yet lost; another Coast Guard surfboat sat on its trailer only feet away from Pentwater Harbor. The Coast Guard could still save the crew of the *Novadoc* and the service's reputation. Chief Boatswain Anderson was in command of this second boat, and he either didn't think to find out where the first surfboat had been launched or, looking over at the *Three Brothers II*, realized there was a more obvious choice for seeking local information. Someone from the second surfboat trotted over to the *Three Brothers II* and asked Clyde Cross his opinion as to the best place to launch the surfboat. Without hesitation Cross pointed out a spot and told the surfboat crewman that site would be deep enough to handle his craft. When the surfboat crew maneuvered the trailer over to the launch site recommended by Cross, Anderson had evidently rethought his options and, for whatever reasons, decided not to launch the surfboat there. Instead, he looked around and found a place he thought was much more suitable for floating his boat. A crewman carefully backed the trailer into the water and someone released the boat. It slid off the trailer and into a mud bank where it stuck like glue.

While what little standing or respect the Coast Guard had within the Pentwater community continued to unravel like a cheap sweater, the *Three Brothers II* had cast off and began making its way out into Lake Michigan. To leave harbor, the little fishing tug had to swing within a few yards of the mud-gripped surfboat and pass under a low bridge. The Coast Guard crew yelled and waved like New Yorkers hailing a taxi. Anderson had also sent a crewman to the top of the bridge, and as the *Three Brothers II* passed under the arch the man leaned way over and from only a few feet away shouted at Cross for help. A funny thing happened. The crew not only didn't hear the Coast Guard's cry for help, they apparently didn't even see them. "Corky" and Joe studiously looked in every direction except toward the point of the compass in which the surfboat rested and Clyde Cross seemed to be preoccupied with something on deck and near his feet. An infuriated Anderson sent a man running back to the Coast Guard Station to get men to push, pull, and manhandle his boat off the mud bank.

Once out on the lake, the crew of the *Three Brothers II* found seas still running unusually high. From the bottom of a trough nothing was visible but sky and water, and to get their bearings the crew had to wait until the fishing tug crested a big comber and take a quick look around before sliding down into the next trough. With an audience on shore cheering him on, Cross handled the old boat like an Olympic equestrian handles a championship horse. He skillfully guided the little boat into the lee side of the *Novadoc* and won at least partial shelter from the waves. Cross then backed the fishing tug within a few inches of the stranded ship, heaved a grappling hook onto the wreck, pulled it taunt and tied off the line to his boat. Clyde then threw his boat into full speed ahead until the line was as taunt as running rigging on a sailing ship, lashed the wheel, and joined Corky and Joe on the tug's roof.

The *Novadoc* crew had watched the little boat draw near, and once she tied onto the wreck they lined up in front of the fishing tug as it rose and fell with each passing wave like an express elevator. Timing the rise and fall of their rescue craft, the sailors wrapped their hands around the line and slid down into the *Three Brothers II*. The fishermen grabbed each new arrival and tossed him into the

For Once in Their Lives, Solid Ground Feels Good

THREE OF THE 17 SEAMEN RESCUED FROM ALMOST CERTAIN DEATH ON THE NOVADOC
Rum and coffee help them to forget the terrors on a ship breaking up on Lake Michigan.

A wire photo showing the Novadoc crewmen the day of their rescue.
Photo courtesy of Lake Superior Maritime Collections, UW – Superior.

cabin and then turned to meet the next sailor. This rite of passage was repeated seventeen times, then the line tying the *Three Brothers II* to the wreck was loosed and the crowded little tug headed for Pentwater.

First Mate Dick Simpell of Midland, Ontario, told the *Ludington Daily News* later that day, "Before we were taken off this morning, I would have given the boat two more hours before she broke completely apart."[46] He proved to be an optimist. Within minutes of the crew leaving the *Novadoc,* it sagged deeper into the water leaving all her decks and some of the superstructure awash.

About halfway back to Pentwater, the *Three Brothers II* met the Coast Guard surfboat that had finally freed itself from the mud and set off in pursuit of the Pentwater fishermen. The surfboat turned and accompanied the fishing tug back to port. What no one realized at the time was that Cross' boat might well be in need of rescuing itself. With twenty men onboard, the boat was very crowded and probably overloaded. Additionally, it was only discovered after she returned to her home port that the gallant old boat came away from the *Novadoc* sporting a hole on her starboard side barely an inch above the waterline. The damage was likely the result of banging up against the wreck during the rescue. It was later determined that various timbers making up the boat's keel were also damaged.

Sometime between being rescued and arriving at the dock in Pentwater, Captain Steip pulled a roll of bills out of his shirt pocket and gestured for Cross to take it. The fisherman refused the offered bankroll and told Steip, "Hell no, Captain. Glad to be of service."[47] Various newspapers reported that after Cross declined the money his crewmen accepted the cash and later split it three ways.

On reaching Pentwater, the *Novadoc* survivors were taken to the U.S. Coast Guard Station, but apparently no first aid was administered and no one assessed the physical condition of the individual crewmen. John Peterson, who was with the two cooks when they died, was in the most serious condition. His feet were badly cut in addition to being pin-cushioned with punctures and still bleeding after soaking for almost two days in icy water. He among all the crew probably suffered the most from hypothermia because he had to either lie down or sit in the water during the length of his stay in the aft cabin. Like the rest of the crew, he was hungry, thirsty, and suffering from exposure. Peterson was taken to the hospital in Hart, Michigan, but there is no record of who took him there. It wasn't the Coast Guard, because they were initially unaware that anyone from the *Novadoc* went to the hospital. The substitute fireman would spend better than two weeks in the small, rural hospital recuperating from his ordeal.

Chief Boatswain Kristofferson was in Ludington and, according to his testimony, didn't receive word until 9:30 A.M. Wednesday morning that survivors had been spotted aboard the *Novadoc*. He immediately left for Pentwater but didn't arrive until after the *Three Brothers II* had brought the shipwrecked sailors ashore. When Kristofferson finally arrived at the Pentwater Coast Guard Station and met the crew of the stricken freighter, he failed to question them about their health or conditions aboard the wreck and neglected to interview Captain Steip before writing his official report of the sinking and rescue.

On Wednesday night, sixteen of the seventeen surviving crew boarded a chartered bus and traveled to Muskegon where they had a two-day layover before catching a Toronto-bound train. By the time Belcher and the rest of the *Novadoc* sailors made it home, bodies from the *Anna C. Minch* had arrived in the Toronto morgue. Lloyd's girlfriend had two brothers who sailed on the *Minch,* and he ended up driving her and her mother to Toronto to possibly identify two of the bodies and make funeral arrangements. When they eventually made it to the morgue, neither of the women could find the strength to go inside, examine the dead, and claim a brother or son. It was left to Lloyd to do.

Relatives and loved ones of the dead and missing sailors from the *William B. Davock* and the *Anna C. Minch* began trickling into Ludington late Wednesday and grew in numbers through the remainder of the week. They came to either identify one of the bodies already recovered or to begin a heavy-hearted and lonely vigil until more bodies came ashore. Although faint hope still flickered in the breasts of some that their loved one might be alive, the locals knew with a certainty none of the missing were still among the living. The Dorrell Funeral Home was swamped with long distance phone calls from anxious and grieving relatives who couldn't make the trip to Ludington but still longed for word of their loved one.

Mrs. C.M. Ferguson of Tipton, Indiana, whose husband served as a fireman on the *William B. Davock*, left immediately for Ludington on hearing the ship had gone down and bodies were washing ashore. On arriving in Grand Rapids, the new widow didn't know what to do after learning there was no immediate bus or train connection to Ludington. When a Michigan State Trooper heard of her predicament, the police officer drove Mrs. Ferguson to Ludington and then drove her back to Grand Rapids when she learned her husband's body wasn't among the known dead.

On Sunday, nearly a week after the *Novadoc* ran aground and broke up, sightseers were still flocking to Jupiter Beach in such numbers they caused traffic jams. Sarnia Steamships, Ltd. hired Clyde Cross to salvage what he could from the wreck, but few

The Novadoc laying nearly submerged following the storm.
Photo courtesy of Lake Superior Maritime Collections, UW – Superior.

people were aware of the business arrangement. Later in the month, two Pentwater men, who were obviously untutored in marine law, decided to claim the wreck by simply rowing out to it and climbing aboard. Everything seemed to be going according to plan until one of the two noticed their rowboat had drifted away and left them stranded. The pair rustled up some sheets which they hung from the wreck hoping somebody on shore would realize people were aboard and needed assistance. And so, the U.S. Coast Guard was called and finally got to rescue somebody from the *Novadoc*.

Captain A.J. Hanna of the Tri Lakes Steamship Company arrived from Chicago on Thursday to inspect the beached *Sinaloa* and determine if the ship was salvageable. He had his doubts. Hanna found the stern and bow bashed in and some steel siding torn from the hull, and he thought the ship had broken her back when it ran aground.

The same day Captain Hanna was examining the "sand sucker," Gladstone police arrested two men who won a free trip to jail charged with piracy. The men, both from Milwaukee, were spotted on the *Sinaloa,* and someone had the presence of mind to write down the license plate number of the car in which they drove off. Gladstone police spotted the car and arrested the duo at 4:00 P.M. Among the valuables from the ship found in their possession were some of the crew's personal effects, a pilot wheel, directional finder, compasses, and $150 in cash.

The company later sent a diver to examine the ship. He found the ship had struck a flat expanse of bedrock and reported he found little structural damage done to the hull. Within a month, the *Sinaloa* was pumped out, refloated, and towed to a dry dock for repairs.

Shortly after being released from the hospital, Captain Fontaine presented the *Sinaloa's* flag to Cecil Shawl and the other Garden Peninsula fishermen who took part in the rescue as a sign of appreciation for their courageous actions in saving his crew.

Chapter 19

"The Thomas F. Cole was Literally Coming Apart at the Seams."

The *Minch,* the *Davock,* and the two fishing tugs out of South Haven had gone down with all hands, and the *Novadoc* was a crumpled pile of junk in which two crew members had lost their lives. As late as two days after the storm had swept up the length of Lake Michigan, it looked like the death toll among Great Lake sailors and the list of ships would continue to grow. Three ships were more than 48 hours overdue, and it was feared they had also been swallowed whole by the storm. Then through the course of the day Wednesday, each of them steamed into port. Almost Jonah-like, they had spent days in the belly of the monster and miraculously survived.

The 251-foot tanker *New Haven Socony* departed Indiana Harbor early Monday morning bound for Muskegon with 600,000 gallons of gasoline, but the ship never made it to the west Michigan port. On Tuesday, evidence of another marine tragedy littered the shore south of Grand Haven when the top of the pilothouse and the wreckage of a lifeboat bearing the name *New Haven Socony,* along with a potpourri of surf-tossed debris, seemed to indicate the storm had claimed another ship. The Associated Press reported on Wednesday that local officials thought the ship might have gone down near Ludington during the storm.

Two days earlier, on leaving port, Captain Harley O. Norton couldn't reconcile what he saw and felt against the few-hours-old weather report calling for strong winds out of the northeast. At the time, the wind was coming from the southeast and, true, the breeze could freshen and swing around to the northeast but, in the captain's experience, storms rarely came from that direction. Like a lot of captains that morning, he opted for caution and took his ship close to the Michigan shore as it steamed north. The tanker had reached a point 25 miles south of Muskegon when the *New Haven Socony's* long ordeal began.

The tanker was barely two hours away from tying up at Muskegon when Captain Norton looked to the southwest and saw dark roiling clouds reaching ahead of a fast approaching dark grey wall. It didn't just look angry, as so many storm fronts are often characterized, it looked malevolent. The captain ordered the helmsman to turn into the wind, and within minutes the ship and crew were fighting for their lives. Tankers ride lower in the water than other bulk carriers making it easier for big seas to inflict damage on the superstructure. Huge rollers—the captain reported that some waves were taller than the boat's 45-foot mast—cascaded over the ship stripping her of lifeboats, railings, deck equipment and ventilators. One monster after another blew in the pilothouse windows, destroyed the compass, and sucked charts out into the maelstrom. The *coup de grâce* came when a huge, curling wall of water climbed over the bow and tore away the pilothouse with Norton and the wheelman inside. Miraculously, both men were left standing unhurt on the now windswept deck.

The wave also damaged the steering mechanism, leaving the ship nearly uncontrollable and in danger of turning broadside to the huge seas. Somehow, the crew rigged emergency steering gear that entailed a lookout on deck shouting orders down a companionway to sailors manipulating machinery in the engine room. It's an art steering a ship from the pilothouse when one can see, feel, and anticipate how the ship will react to wind and wave, but to do it by relaying information to crewmen grappling with emergency apparatus in the bowels of the vessel during a raging storm seems all but impossible. The radio-telephone had disappeared along with the pilothouse, and then the heating plant went kaput. The latter didn't endanger the ship, it just made the crew that much more miserable in the 10-degree above zero temperature. Down in the wildly gyrating inferno, otherwise known as the boiler room, the crew kept the fires going—if they died, so did the ship.

For two days, the *New Haven Socony* stayed afloat and met the storm head on. The battle for survival kept the men at their

Last Boat of the Season, Sarnia, Ontario.—19.

Post card from 1954 illustrating how much ice can accumulate on a ship during a storm.

From the author's post card collection.

posts for the entire 48 hours and left them bruised, battered, groggy from lack of sleep, hungry, and overloaded with stress. As the hours ticked by and wave after wave beat against the tanker, a new threat arose—ice. Every wave that came aboard or showered the tanker's superstructure in spray laid down another thin layer of ice. After two days, the *New Haven Socony* was encrusted in better than two inches of ice. Add to that the weight of the water which had wormed its way into the holds, and the ship's continued buoyancy came into question.

The battle with the storm had turned the *New Haven Socony* into a floating wreck by the time it limped into East Chicago's harbor on Wednesday. The tanker was so weighed down in ice there was barely 18 inches of freeboard between the deck and Lake Michigan. Captain Norton was of the opinion his ship was within an hour of foundering when it reached port. Boatswain Frank Myers reflecting on the extraordinary events of the past two days told reporters, "We've been through hell and we've been practically all over Lake Michigan. But here we are okay."[48]

The 580-foot *Thomas F. Cole*, built in 1907 in Ecorse, Michigan, has been called an unlucky ship. She ran aground in 1910 in the St. Mary's River and sustained major damage. Then on May 13, 1913, the *Cole* rammed the barge *Iron City* on Lake St. Clair and cut it in two. Again in the St. Mary's River in 1964 a British freighter collided with the *Cole* that sent the ore carrier to Lorain, Ohio, for repairs. However, if you had asked any of the crew who sailed the *Thomas F. Cole* during the Armistice Day Storm about her luck, they probably would have vowed to a man the old "straight deck" was the luckiest boat on the Lakes.

The *Cole* was preparing to leave Gary, Indiana, early Monday morning when a clerk called Captain Parson's attention to a storm warning posted by the Weather Bureau in Chicago. The posting warned of strong winds out of the northeast, but the captain felt no great concern over the forecast. Still, Parsons played it safe, and when the *Cole* left harbor at 4:00 A.M., he took his ship up the eastern shore of Lake Michigan. By 10:00 A.M. the winds were flexing their muscles and blowing with authority. Around noon, the captain noticed the wind direction had begun to rotate around until it was blowing from the southwest and the old sailor felt instinctively a bad blow was in the offing. He quickly made the decision to get off the lee shore and take the ore carrier to the big lake's western shore.

As the storm abruptly built to full crescendo, the men in the pilothouse, 55 feet above the waterline, often had to look up to see the tops of the waves. Then, out of the spray-besmeared gloom, came a series of massive combers that lifted the *Cole's* bow out of the water and allowed the wind, which packed the power of a freight train, to slam into the great expanse of exposed steel and pushed the ship around until it was pointing to the northeast. The wheelman tried several times to bring the ship back on a westward heading, but the engine couldn't overpower the one-two punch of wind and wave.

The *Cole* was in a fix that left Captain Parsons with only two options, both of which came with serious drawbacks. The ship could continue on a northeast course and run before the storm. That the ship would soon run out of lake and hit the Michigan coastline, a la the *Novadoc*, took the bloom off this option. Or, Parsons could let the boat wallow in the troughs between the waves and hopefully ride out the storm there. The *Cole* might even be able to make some leeway, meaning it would stay in the troughs while steaming to the west and putting a little sea room between itself and Michigan's mitten. At the best, this option meant the *Cole* would be subjected to a lot of rolling and a severe beating. At the worse, the ship would begin a roll, never recover, and capsize. Parsons choose the second option and warned his crew to prepare for an uncomfortable and dangerous ride.

So began a marathon of misery. Waves might not be engulfing the bow and jolting the entire ship, but the *Cole* rolled continuously as the huge combers passed under her. With every roll, the crew waited to see how far over the old boat would go and whether or not the *Cole* would recover and begin a wild swing in the opposite direction. As the ship rolled, the broken off tops of great waves continued to batter the freighter and at one point waves broke over the stern with such force they hammered the iron plating making up the outer shell of the after cabins into scrap. Water poured into the breech and put the ship's telephone out of order and flooded the boiler room until it was almost knee-deep in icy water. The violent rolls broke open a barrel of oil in the boiler room and gilded the ice cold water in an oil slick. Muscling one shovel full of coal after another into a boiler's fire box under the conditions aboard the *Cole* deserved to be ranked as one of Dante's inner circles of Hell. As hard as it was to throw coal into a small opening from a pitching deck, the job called for more than just timing, brute muscle and endurance. Each shovel full had to be placed precisely in the right spot to maintain a bed of fire free of either cold or hot spots. With cold water lapping at their knees, the deck rolling as much as 40 degrees from one side to another, an oily slick slowly spreading over everything, and the stress of wondering if the next minute could be their last, the firemen aboard the *Cole* had to throw a load of coal into a fire box with the accuracy of champion dart thrower.

While this was going on below deck, waves were carrying away life lines, railings, and entombing the deck lights in a foot of ice. No one went on deck for a day and a half, and the crew in the forward section of the ship went without food or coffee.

The ceaseless rolling continued throughout the night, and when the sky lightened Tuesday morning, Parsons discovered his ship was perilously close to the Michigan coastline. Even while being rocked by the endless ranks of waves arriving from the southwest, the crew began to detect a counter rhythm as the water pushed up on the eastern shore flowed back into the lake creating a backset of waves. The captain ordered the rudder put 35 degrees to port and to his surprise and relief the ship responded and settled on a north northwest course. For hours, the *Cole* held to the course and at last began to put some sea room between itself and the Lower Peninsula. Still, the ship sailed parallel to the waves. To those on board it felt like they were being rocked by a madman.

The wind significantly eased about 5:00 P.M. Tuesday, and by 5:30 Parson was able to point the long suffering ship and its crew into the wind. As night fell, the wind continued to back off and by 10 in the evening Parsons judged it safe to venture out on deck. Freed from the bridge, he set out to assess the damage to his ship. The captain's first stop, the galley, had undergone an extraordinarily violent transformation over the past 36 hours. The ship's extreme rolling had torn the large stove from its moorings and tossed it around the galley like dice shaken in a cup. It pulverized cabinets, ripped out fixtures, and chewed the room's oak paneling from the walls and left hardly a piece of it bigger than a toothpick. The storage room, ice box, pantry, and dining room were all smashed with food, plates, pots and pans, water, and various unidentifiable bits and pieces scattered across the floor in a Mulligan's Stew of wreckage. Two crew members were slightly hurt, and a steward couldn't be found and hadn't been seen since clearing Gary. The same seas that had bashed in the aft cabin's iron plating swept away doors leading to the engine room which allowed more of Lake Michigan to fully explore various below-deck compartments. The addition of the oil from the broken barrel left much of the engine room in a nightmare of goo.

The real heart-stopper came when the seasoned captain inspected the cargo hold. Hundreds of rivet heads lay everywhere as mute testimony to the severity of the storm and raised ominous questions concerning the ship's continued and even immediate

Post Card of the Thomas F. Cole.
From the author's post card collection.

survival. The violent rolling had put the hull under such enormous stress the rivets holding the hull plates together had popped. The plates in the hold moved back and forth with the motion of the ship as it headed into the wind and met the waves. On deck, Parsons spied more popped off rivet heads under the foot of ice that blanketed everything. Five-hundred feet long iron ships flex like a skyscraper in a high wind and can even be seen to slightly twist in heavy seas, but Captain Parsons realized the *Cole* had more than a noticeable sag amidships accompanied by a pronounced and permanent twist in the hull. The *Thomas F. Cole* was literally coming apart at the seams! The captain ordered speed reduced to slow.

The *Cole* entered the port of Milwaukee at 6:00 A.M. Wednesday morning. She had been at sea for 50 hours and on reaching Milwaukee was barely 100 miles, by sea, from Gary, Indiana. The captain went ashore to call the home office and on his return learned the lost steward had been rescued from a barrel of asbestos in which he had become stuck. With a wrecked galley, Parsons took most of the crew to a restaurant for breakfast. It was their first meal in over two days. With full bellies, one detail attacked the galley and dining room with shovels while most of the crew turned steam lines and water hoses on the mini glaciers covering the decks. As the ice receded, it became all the more apparent that the huge seas had strained the *Cole's* hull until it started shedding rivets like a wriggling dog sheds water.

The American Bureau of Shipping surveyed the damaged boat and within days Parsons was ordered to sail the *Cole* to the American Shipyard dry dock in South Chicago and to do so with, "extreme caution."⁴⁹ It took the rest of the winter to repair the ship.

Captain Robert W. Parsons claimed it wasn't skilled seamanship that saved his ship. In his humble opinion what got the *Thomas F. Cole* safely into Milwaukee harbor was plain and simply, "a miracle."⁵⁰

⌖

As Wednesday drew to a close, fears mounted that Lake Michigan may have claimed the package freighter *Alfred H. Smith* and her crew. The 381-foot-long ship had been due in Milwaukee on Tuesday and was last seen Monday passing through the Straits of Mackinac, only a 20-hour run from the Wisconsin port. While officials of the Great Lakes Transit Corp. and friends and loved ones of the crew wondered and worried Wednesday night and into Thursday morning, the freighter edged closer to Milwaukee and the end of a memorable journey.

The voyage began on November 9 when the ship departed Buffalo, New York, with a mixed cargo, stopped briefly in Erie, Pennsylvania, to take on more freight, and again in Windsor, Ontario. At Detroit, the crew loaded forty-one cars and trucks on board and chained them down as deck cargo. It was just another ordinary and uneventful trip for the general cargo hauler that had been moving the manufacturing wealth of the Midwest and the world to and from Great Lake ports since her launching in 1907.

Near the midway point between Beaver Island and South Fox Island, the *Smith* plowed into the storm and the voyage went from run-of-the-mill to extraordinary in a matter of minutes. Captain Healy had spent a lifetime on the Great Lakes; he had served as lake captain for 22 years and skippered the *Alfred H. Smith* since 1932. He had been caught on the lakes during the great 1905 blow and survived the 1913 storm. In his opinion, neither of the two previous super storms matched in severity to what he experienced over the next two days.

Wind and seas pounded the ship unmercifully, and Captain Healy didn't even care to guess the height of the waves. The dropping temperatures glazed the deck in ice, and with the ship staggering every few seconds under the heavy impact of the on-coming seas, the vehicles began to break loose from their tie-downs and skid wildly across the deck. Healy told the *Milwaukee Journal*, "The deck became a skating rink, and the cars began to slide. Long as I live, I'll never forget the clanking of those sliding cars hitting each other, their fenders banging as the lashings and blocks gave way."[51]

The captain decided survival depended on returning to Mackinaw City and put his ship about. In turning 180 degrees, the *Smith* lost two cars and a truck overboard and began listing at a 45 degree angle. The storm put the front spotlight out-of-order followed closely by the main compass in the pilothouse which toppled from its stand and crashed onto the deck. As a last resort, the wheelman and captain manned the emergency wheel atop the pilothouse. During all this wild pitching and change in direction that sent cars careening around the deck like a mad pinball game, the crew were on hands and knees on that icy deck and among the caroming cars risking their lives to tie them down. From the top of the pilothouse Healy noticed a 600-foot ore carrier was paralleling their course and also steaming for the shelter of the Straits. The captain watched the "straight deck" roll so far over he though she was going under, but the ship somehow righted itself and both boats made it to Mackinaw City where the *Smith* let go both bow anchors and spent the night.

The next day it took six hours for the ship to get underway because the anchor lines had fouled overnight. Wednesday they again left the Straits of Mackinac behind and limped toward Milwaukee. When the ship arrived in port, she presented an unusual sight. Automobiles lay every which way on deck with some of them canted over the ship's sides as if they were trying to escape the madness the *Smith* had had to endure. Below decks, the *Smith's* freight had been transformed into a surreal and sticky mess. Nine hundred seventy-three refrigerators had shed their restraints and tumbled together at the bottom of the hold until they were reduced to coils, refrigerant, shelving, broken doors, and large, misshapen crypts. The now useless scrap was slathered in the contents of better than a thousand burst cans of sardines—whether oil or water-packed was not specified. This was topped off by a coating of chocolate syrup with here and there a piece of miscellaneous freight serving as a Maraschino cherry. Ahh, a sundae only Salvador Dali could appreciate. Other than bumps and black-and-blue bruises from the inevitable falls on the icy decks, none of the crew were seriously injured. Captain Healy, who had sailed the Great Lakes for 37 years called the two-day ordeal, "The most harrowing experience of my life."[52]

Chapter 20

"Reiser was Surprised Everyone Survived the Night."

The number of fatalities among duck hunters along the Mississippi continued to rise Wednesday as more bodies arrived at funeral homes in towns along the upper Mississippi. Pilot Bob Bean, a flier with the Max Conrad Flying Service, spent all day conducting an aerial survey of three areas along the great river in the Winona area. He reported lots of abandoned boats, a marooned dog, but no sign of any stranded hunters. Across the river and a few miles north in Wisconsin, boats, outboard motors, and even shotguns picked up by the tug *Thockmorton*, on a sweep that day of the Winona Pool, had all been dropped off at the Fountain City boatyard and waited to be claimed.

More than 100 miles to the south on the Mississippi at Prairie du Chien, four ducks hunters who had spent more than 48 cold, miserable hours in the Mississippi wetlands finally made it to safety. Robert Reiser, 31, told of the group's near fatal hunting trip that began rather benignly at 5:00 A.M. on Monday morning. Robert and three other hunting buddies left home in a light mist. The quartet was well out in the river when the storm struck with an intensity and suddenness that none in the group had ever experienced. Within a dip of a paddle, Reiser said, "… there were white caps on the river and the waves were higher than I have ever seen them before."[53] It got so cold they tried to light a fire in their canoe using gasoline and decoys, but the decoys proved flame resistant. It was impossible or suicidal to cross open water in the canoe, so the foursome spent the night in the river's backwater huddled in the bottom of the aluminum boat. Unable to even stand let alone walk around and stomp their feet in the intense cold, Reiser was surprised everyone survived the night. And then fate dealt them a reprieve.

The party was close to freezing to death on Tuesday when a boater stumbled across the hunters. Their rescuer took the four to his houseboat where he tried to get some hot coffee in the men, but their hands shook so violently from the cold they couldn't get the java in their mouths before their tremors emptied the cups. The houseboat evidently had no heater because on Tuesday night the men stomped around the houseboat on feet they couldn't feel and beat their arms trying to stay warm and awake. Wednesday, a rescue party found the hunters and returned them to Prairie du Chien.

From Prairie du Chien to Redwing, Minnesota search parties were out again Thursday looking for the missing. It was more a recovery operation now than a rescue mission, and the nagging question on most officials minds' was how many more victims were still out there. The many snow-covered cars found near hunting grounds or boat launching sites continued to worry state and local police and safety officials because no one knew if the vehicles belonged to hunters who had found other means of reaching home or represented still more hunters lost and unaccounted for.

Even as the death toll continued to mount and the search parties went about the grim task of recovering bodies, other hunters on Wednesday grabbed sack of decoys, shotguns, called to their Lab, and headed for the very pools where others had died only two days before and from which not all the bodies had been recovered. The snow-covered remains of two hunters were inadvertently discovered by a couple of buddies hoping to bag some waterfowl. Wednesday's trickle of hunters grew steadily through Thursday and reached full flow Friday as duck hunters, undeterred by a death toll on the stretch of river lying between Red Wing and Prairie du Chien that stood at twenty, streamed back into the Mississippi bottomlands in search of their limit.

It was a powerful demonstration of the emotional and/or biological forces working in some people that pulled them out to a duck blind in spite of god awful weather and recent tragedy. To non-duck hunters, those forces are as inexplicable as the magnetic field surrounding the planet.

Snowplow and men with shovels attempt to clear a road after the Armistice Day blizzard.
Photo courtesy of the Minnesota Historical Society.

In Minneapolis/St. Paul, schools were still closed Wednesday, and traffic in the Twin Cities and throughout the state was still pretty much at a standstill. For instance, milk delivery within the Twin Cities on Tuesday had been reduced by 85% and Wednesday that had improved to the point where deliveries to homes and stores had reached 50% of pre-storm levels. Even that meant a lot of fathers were out trudging through the snow in order to feed their children, and a lot of breakfast cereal was being eaten dry. Thousands of downtown office workers were desperate to get home after bedding down for two nights in hallways and ballrooms.

On Tuesday, more than a thousand transit company employees had hit the streets with shovels and worked at clearing streetcar tracks. They must have only scraped off the top layer of snow because on Wednesday Minneapolis radio stations put out the word that the streetcar company was hiring men to shovel snow. Job seekers showed up from all over the Twin Cities, some having walked for hours, and jammed the company offices. Five hundred were hired to dig out the trolleys, and several hundred more went home without jobs.

Conditions were decidedly worse out in the country. Bernard J. Luhman farmed near Howard Lake, Minnesota. He had spent all day Tuesday and most of Wednesday morning doing chores and waiting for the phone to ring. Luhman was one of the county's plowmen, and the call finally came at noon on Wednesday to report to the plow shed that held the Caterpillar tractor and plow. It was an exhausting one-mile walk away. He and his partner spent until 3:00 P.M. the next afternoon attaching the plow and getting the Cat ready to work. They then plowed non-stop for the next 24 hours. On Friday, after 56 hours of work, Bernard and his co-worker turned the plow over to a relief crew. For the next two weeks, Lehman and his partner were one of three teams that worked an eight-hour daily shift clearing all county roads. The pay for the first 56-hour shift cleared Bernard $19.60 or 35 cents an hour.

One hundred cars and twice that number of men, women, and children poured into Glencoe, Minnesota, 40 miles west of Minneapolis, after finally being freed from snowdrifts two miles west of town. Most of the people had been trapped in their cars since early Tuesday. Many were suffering from cold and exposure, but there were surprisingly few serious injuries. One of the worst was a pair of badly frost-bitten hands. The crowd quickly filled Glencoe's cafes and stores looking for food and warmth while waiting for the highway department plows to clear routes out of town.

Highway workers clearing Highway 169 south of Belle Plaine in south central Minnesota discovered two more storm victims at the bottom of a 12-foot snowdrift. The tragedy began when Mr. Carleton Saltzman of Minneapolis stalled his car in calf-high snow on Monday. John Ahrens, a nearby farmer, offered his house as a refuge, but Saltzman declined saying he'd wait in his car for a plow to come along. When a neighbor told Ahrens that two travelers had taken shelter in his house, Ahrens thought one of them must be Saltzman. The second body in the car belonged to a man who had become stuck near Saltzman and joined him in waiting for a plow. The men died of carbon monoxide poisoning. The plow arrived two days later. The tip of Saltzman's car's radio antenna was just visible at the top of the snow bank, the only hint of what lay beneath.

By Thursday, Minnesota Highway Department crews had opened at least one lane of traffic on nearly all major roads but notified the public that it was not yet safe to travel by car in the state. Still new tragedies were coming to light. The bodies of two brothers, John Garrison, 20, and 15-year-old Charles were found in a swamp near Sauk Centre, a hundred miles northwest of the Twin Cities, on Thursday. The 24-hour search for the Garrisons began when a snowplow discovered their abandoned truck.

From the condition and position of the bodies, rescuers believe the brothers were attempting to walk to safety after their truck became stuck. Charles must have become ill or simply exhausted because it appears John was carrying his younger brother when he stepped in a post hole and broke his leg. When death stole over them, John was on top of Charles with his arms under his younger brother as if he was carrying him. It is not known how long the two brothers lay huddled together before the storm took their lives.

Turkey farmers across Minnesota, on Thursday, asked Republican Governor Harold E. Stassen to postpone Thanksgiving Day for one week. The storm had virtually wiped out those birds just ready for market, and the turkey raisers said they needed a week to get other birds ready to process. The request was denied. Turkey prices increased 1.5 cents a pound wholesale at the Chicago Mercantile Exchange.

If the turkeys didn't get to the dinner table, they did get to the Minneapolis Hide and Tallow Company. Usually the company collected meat scraps, bones, and grease from area restaurants and grocery stores, applied heat to the mess, and rendered out the fat. A week after the storm, turkey growers had dropped off a half million frozen turkeys at the plant. It took until spring for the plant to whittle down the mountain of frozen gobblers and process the last of the birds.

By week's end, trolleys were once again running in Minneapolis/St. Paul, and nearly all schools were open. The hunt for bodies continued through the weekend with at least six hunters missing and unaccounted for. It would be weeks before all state and county roads were cleared of snow and open to traffic.

FRIDAY
&
BEYOND

Chapter 21

"The Three Sailors
Have Never Been Identified."

Clyde Cross bested the Coast Guard again on Friday, November 15 when he discovered the final resting place of the *Anna C. Minch*. The inquisitive and adventurous fisherman with the heart of a St. Bernard and his crew cast off from the Pentwater dock and headed out into Lake Michigan at 8:00 A.M. as he said, "To scout around and see what we could see."[54] After failing to find anything of interest in three hours of "scouting," Cross turned the *Three Brothers II* toward home when he spotted what he first thought was a seagull resting on the water. There was something about whatever he saw that just didn't fit, so he steered the old tug for a closer inspection. The seagull turned out to be the tip of a mast just breaking the surface of the water and flying a wind-direction pennant. Peering beneath the water, Cross could see the ghostly silhouette of a drowned ship attached to the other end of the mast. The ship was lying in 40 feet of water roughly 1.75 miles south southwest of the Pentwater breakwater light and approximately 0.75 miles from the beach. Cross detached the pennant and brought it to Pentwater where representatives from Sarnia Steamships Ltd., owners of the *Anna C. Minch*, took one look at the triangular flag and announced it came from their lost ship.

Cross was hired by the *Minch's* owners to survey the position of the wreck and arrange for the recovery of bodies, of which nineteen could still be aboard. The first diver to inspect the wreck went in the water in late November. He reported finding a gaping hole on the *Minch's* port side running from the bilge to the deck just aft of the forward cargo hold. The pilothouse, forward deck, railings, and the forward cabins were all missing as if scrubbed clean from the hull. Also missing was a 120-foot-long aft section of the ship that included the crew's quarters. The diver couldn't locate the stern in two days of searching. Further exploration of the wreck was halted by bad weather.

The wreckage spoke of the horrendous violence inflicted on the Canadian ship, and most experts felt the evidence, particularly the large gash near the bow, indicated the *Anna C. Minch* went down as a result of a collision, probably with the *William B. Davock*. The mystery of the missing stern section wouldn't be solved for months until it was discovered lying in slightly deeper water 600 feet from the rest of the hull. The aft section had also been swept clean of cabins, railings, and vents. As late as 1960, when scuba diver Louis R. Desperes reported on his exploration of the stern half of the *Minch* in an article for *Skin Diver Magazine,* he wrote as if there was no doubt that the *William B. Davock* had collided with the *Minch* and cut the ship in two. For Desperes, the primary evidence pointing to a collision was that the *Minch* lay on the bottom in two pieces. Almost from the night of the storm, many veteran sailors thought the *Davock* and *Minch* had collided, but until the *Davock* was found and examined, opinions would remain opinions and certainty would go begging—and the *Davock* was in no hurry to reveal herself.

The pennant found by Clyde Cross now rests in the Huron Institute in Collingwood, Ontario, the hometown from which six of the *Anna C. Minch's* crewmen hailed. Today, zebra mussels encrust the *Minch,* and waves and ice continue the destruction Lake Michigan began in 1940.

⌐₫⌐

With the discovery of the *Minch,* the search for the *William B. Davock* intensified. Since bodies from the two ships washed ashore at approximately the same time, although miles apart, searchers began thinking that the *Davock* might not be any farther off shore than the *Anna C. Minch.* And because most of the bodies from the *Davock* came ashore 10 to 15 miles north of those from the *Minch,* searchers began looking closer ashore in the Ludington area. Representatives of the Interlakes Steamship Co. boarded the thirty-foot tug *Mary K* in Ludington on Friday and conducted a search in what they thought were the likely waters where the *Davock* went down. They found nothing. Interlakes then asked that a thorough search of the

Lake Michigan coastline between Oceana and Mason County lines be undertaken. It was conducted Sunday the seventeenth without any new discoveries coming to light.

On Friday, November 15, 1940, at Lorain, Ohio, 19-year-old Sterling Wood was laid to rest. The deckhand from the *William B. Davock* was the first of the victims to be returned home and buried. He would never claim the $200 scholarship from Baldwin-Wallace College and never realize his dream of getting a higher education. The day after the funeral, another body, later identified as that of Frank Stanek, a 36-year-old wheelman on the *Davock*, washed ashore near Big Sable Point Lighthouse. A third body was found on Sunday morning on the southern edge of Ludington State Park. The body was that of Lawrence D. Gonyea of Cloquet, Minnesota. Gonyea, 23, served as a deck steward aboard the *Davock*. Neither body wore a life jacket, and each was clad in only light clothing suggesting both men were in their bunks or rooms when the *Davock* went to the bottom and had neither time to dress nor even don a life preserver. A week after the storm, Clyde Cross was still spending his days on the *Three Brothers II* searching the waters for the *Davock*.

A few days later, three Great Lakes sailors were buried together at the Lakeview Cemetery in Ludington under a small monument honoring the crews of the *William B. Davock* and the *Anna C. Minch*. The three bodies have never been identified, and it proved impossible to even match one of the bodies to one of the two ships. The memorial was paid for by the Interlakes Steamship Company.

The wreckage of the *Davock* was finally discovered in May 1972, off Little Sable Point in 204 feet of water by Kent Bellrichard, John Steele, and William Cohrs using high-tech sonar gear. A brief exploratory dive found the ship resting upside down, and none of the three divers found any evidence that the *Davock* had been involved in a collision. They did find a significant clue to the ship's demise. The *Davock's* rudder was found turned hard to port suggesting the bulk hauler and her crew found themselves parallel to the waves and rolling heavily in the huge seas. The captain would have ordered the rudder hard to port in a desperate attempt to bull his ship out of a trough and into the face of the storm. Either the ship was unable to power her way into the seas or the *Davock* rolled too far to recover and capsized before she could break out of the trough.

Robert Younkins was six when his father Floyd died aboard the *Davock*. His dad's body was never recovered although there had been a brief fleeting hope when an unidentified body thought to be Floyd's came ashore. Robert's grandfather traveled to Ludington to view the body of the unknown sailor only to find it wasn't his son. As such, there had never been a funeral or closure for the Younkins family. Thirteen years later, Robert applied for a job with Interlakes Steamship Company. When the company was informed that Robert was the son of a man who was lost on the *Davock*, he got the job. It was a good job in 1953, but maybe it was also a way for Robert to connect with a father who was taken from him when he was just a young child.

Charles Findlay, the man who joined the crew of the *Davock* for one voyage because he was eager to get off sick leave and start earning some money never returned home. The last his wife and two girls, Joyce, 8, and Jane, 4, saw of Charles was when he hopped on a trolley and waved goodbye. He expected to be gone maybe a week; instead, he was gone forever. His body was never found. There was never a real last farewell. It was a loss that left a hole in the heart, so 62 years later the youngest daughter of Charles Findley stood on the Lake Michigan beach, near where the *Davock* went down and a few feet away from a Michigan Historical Marker that recounts the Armistice Day Storm, and took comfort in the beauty of the view and the nearby plaque memorializing the men lost on November 11, 1940.

In addition to the lives of the fishermen on the *Richard H.* and the *Indian*, the storm had a devastating effect on commercial fishing throughout the Great Lakes. Docks, nets, buildings, and boats were damaged or destroyed with the losses mounting into the thousands of dollars. The financial hit put many fishermen out of business. The *Great Lakes Journal* reported that most banks would not accept fishing boats as collateral for loans to commercial fishermen who needed to buy new nets and equipment. Lake Erie fishermen predicted the coming season would prove to be the poorest in the previous sixteen years because of the damage to their nets.

On June 2, 2003, Michigan Shipwreck Research Associates, using side-viewing sonar, discovered a hulk the size of a school bus lying on the bottom of Lake Michigan near the spot where the *Richard H.* was last seen and is believed to have gone down. As of this writing, no one has yet descended to the wreck to confirm its identity.

Chapter 22

"Finding Of Facts."

Letters of complaint from public, church, and community leaders, captains of industry, and even congressmen began finding their way to the Coast Guard almost before the *Three Brothers II* landed the crew of the *Novadoc* at Pentwater. The whole affair put the service in a poor light, and it didn't take long for the Coast Guard to respond. On November 25, 1940, a Board of Investigation convened at Pentwater Station, "To inquire into the facts and circumstances connected with the loss of lives from the steamships *Novadoc*, *W. B. Davock*, and *Anna C. Minch* during the storm of 11 and 12 November 1940."[55] Chief Boatswain Alfred E. Kristofferson was named as a defendant, and the board advised him to retain a lawyer. He declined.

After several days of testimony from U.S. Coast Guard personnel, the crew of the *Three Brothers II*, and other locals, the Board of Investigation issued their Finding of Facts. Among the findings, the Board declared that:

A.E. Kristofferson had not issued the required orders to his subordinate.

A.E. Kristofferson remained out of direct communication with developments concerning the wreck of the *Novadoc*.

There was a woodland road that would have made it possible get the beach apparatus cart closer to the *Novadoc*.

Beach apparatus could have been delivered to the beach but wasn't.

Assistance in many forms was volunteered but none was accepted.

Winds moderated significantly after midnight on November 13.

A.E. Kristofferson failed to interview surviving members of the *Novadoc.*

If the Board's Finding of Facts wasn't bad enough, the opinion of the court was even more damning. It stated that the beach apparatus should have been at the wreck site and the breeches buoy deployed. A motor S-B Surfboat should have made an attempt to leave Pentwater on the twelfth and reach the *Novadoc.* In spite of the hazards and based on the experience of previous rescues under similar conditions, a rescue could have been accomplished during the daylight hours of November 12. Furthermore, Alfred M. Anderson lacked confidence and experience and failed to assume the responsibilities he was delegated. On the other hand, the Board was of the opinion that Chief Boatswain Kristofferson failed to show good leadership, judgment, or initiative.

The Board recommended that A.E. Kristofferson, a past recipient of the Gold Life-Saving Medal, be relieved of his duties at Ludington and be assigned to a single unit command. It was recommended that Alfred M. Anderson be assigned an additional year as acting rating before being considered for permanent promotion and that he be transferred to a more active unit where he could gain experience. On December 23, 1940, the Coast Guard Commander of the Chicago District reviewed but did not approve the Board's recommendations concerning Kristofferson because the transfer would only result in, "adverse publicity for the service."[56] The recommendations for Alfred Anderson were approved. The commander of the district noted after a review of the proceedings that there was a general, "...failure of personnel to be properly indoctrinated in their duties."[57] Then and now, the U.S. Coast Guard expects the impossible to be matter-of-factly accomplished.

During the proceedings, a lone voice spoke out for Chief Boatswain Kristofferson. Leland H. Kent of the Pere Marquette Railroad Company spoke for his company and for many of the men who sailed the Great Lakes when, at the end of his questioning, the Board asked if he wished to make a statement. Kent did, and in part said, "At this time I want again to reiterate the necessity for the *Escanaba* being prepared for fall and winter storms. It looks silly and asinine to send a boat of this caliber which could outlive any storm and has equipment aboard to render assistance, to a shipyard in late fall and let her sit there for months till she pretty near takes root to a dock, and then criticize someone else that has done more than their share."[58]

There are conflicting stories as to the eventual end of the *Three Brothers II.* Corky Fisher claimed Clyde sold the boat not long after the rescue and within two years of the sale it ran aground near Sleeping Bear Dunes and was a total loss. Government records, however, show that the *Three Brothers II* was owned by Clyde Cross until 1950. Cross said that after he sold the boat it burned at sea taking the lives of three sailors.

Clyde Cross moved to California in 1949 for his health and crewed on tuna boats before hiring onto a shrimp boat in South America. He ended his days managing an apartment complex in California. In later years he down-played his daring rescue saying he was just, "... doing something to help."[59] The Canadian government presented Cross with a silver engraved plate in appreciation for rescuing the *Novadoc's* crew. Cross died in 2002, his two crewmen had preceded him in death.

Corky Fisher was born in 1909 and after a lifetime of adventures returned to his hometown. Corky lived into his eighties and spent several hours a day chopping firewood in order to work the kinks out of his aging but still robust frame. When Lloyd Belcher returned to Pentwater in 1984 with his wife and camped at Charles Mears State Park, Corky was one of the first to visit the former *Novadoc* crewman. Joe Fountain moved to Detroit sometime after the storm and dropped out of sight and history.

Wheelman Lloyd Belcher had no trouble holding a true course through life after his experiences on the *Novadoc.* Although Belcher faced the possibility of eminent extinction huddled in the cold, dark wreck with his fellow crewmen, he was alone with his thoughts. The young man turned to prayer, and when he survived the night, the next day, and the next night, he thanked the Lord and promised he would always sing his praises. For the next 65 years, the wheelman never forgot his promise. He sang in the church choir and held true to the course he found that night.

Belcher tried to give up the sea, but he sailed for another six months on the Great Lakes and then joined the Canadian Navy. He was a wheelman on a warship guarding the western approaches to the English Channel when a German bomb struck his ship not fifteen feet from where he was manning the wheel. The bomb sliced through the deck and plunged into the engine room before exploding. Belcher escaped injury and after the war returned home to find work on terra firma. He died in 2006.

Today, the *Novadoc* lies flattened on the lake bottom in shallow water off Pentwater's Juniper Beach. It is a popular destination for beginning scuba divers.

Locally famous throughout the Midwest, young Liberace left for New York shortly after the Winona concert in search of wider recognition and fame. He found it.

In the Lake Carrier Association's 1941 annual report, it was noted that the association paid out $6,325 in death benefits to relatives of seamen who lost their lives in 1940 while in the performance of their ship's duty.

After the storm, the *Great Lakes Journal* called for a Coast Guard station on the north shore of Lake Michigan pointing out that the southern coastline of the Upper Peninsula is, "one of the longest stretches of shoreline on the Great Lakes without a coast guard station, patrol boat, or cutter..."[59] The journal also suggested it, "should be mandatory for all steamship companies to equip their ships with either ship-to-shore telephones or wireless systems."[60]

In the wake of the storm, all major weather bureaus in major cities across the country were staffed 24-7. Regional offices were also given the responsibility for forecasting the weather in their region.

The ore-carrier *Henry Steinbrenner,* which sailed through the same patch of Lake Michigan at roughly the same time the storm sent the *Davock* and *Minch* to the bottom, continued to crease the waters of the upper lakes for another thirteen years. On May 10, 1953, the old "straight deck" sailed from Superior, Wisconsin, in calm weather on a flat Lake Superior, with local weather forecasts predicting winds of up to 35 mph. The *Steinbrenner* was only hours into its voyage when a storm came out of nowhere, and by 11:00 P.M. winds screamed across the big lake at 80 mph. With no foul weather expected, the captain had been slow in ordering the hatch-cover hold-down bolts tightened and the canvas hatch covers secured. The crew worked through the night, but wind and wave pried loose the coverings before they could be completely secured, and water began entering the hull.

The mounting seas swept across the ship with such power and regularity it became impossible to set foot on deck, and by 7:30 A.M. the ship's pumps couldn't keep up with the incoming water. The captain ordered the engines stopped, sent out SOS calls, and sounded the abandon ship whistle. All thirty-one crewmen made it into the two lifeboats and a life raft they had managed to launch, but it would be over four hours before help arrived. During that interminable wait, the lifeboats and raft were repeatedly overturned by mountainous seas, and with each cruel baptism in the lake, fewer men found the strength and will to fight their way back into the boats or the raft. When, after Herculean efforts by the U.S. Coast Guard and remarkable feats of seamanship by several lake freighters, help arrived on the scene, only fourteen survivors were pulled from a lake that can be as beautiful as she is unforgiving. As always, the Great Lakes require sailors to be ever alert, always careful, and make decisions at the speed of light.

The Armistice Day Storm is indelibly etched in the memory of every living Minnesotan who was older than a toddler and resided in the state on November 11, 1940. Considering the stories of hardship, adventure, tragedy, and near providential survival associated with the storm were told and retold by those who experienced it, many natives of the great state belonging to the baby boomer generation have second-hand memories that are almost as vivid as those who lived through the maelstrom.

Max Conrad became one of the world's greatest light aircraft pilots. His remarkable career included 200 solo flights across the Atlantic or Pacific and the training of 3,000 pilots. He set many impressive long distance flying records in light planes, many of which have never been matched or bested. In 1954 he followed Lindberg's route across the Atlantic and became the second man in history to fly solo from New York to Paris. In 1961, he set the world record for a westbound around-the-world solo flight in a light plane. The flight took ten days and the record still stands. In an attempt to fly around the world via the poles, Conrad was the first civilian to land a plane at the South Pole; he was 67 at the time. On taking off from the pole, he crashed and destroyed his plane, but Max was unhurt. The airport at Winona, Minnesota, is named Max Conrad Field.

Members of the Minnesota Meteorological Society consider the Armistice Day Storm of 1940 as one of the top five weather events of the twentieth century in the state. The Minnesota Climatology Office ranks it number two in the state's top five weather events of the twentieth century. The Dust Bowl holds down the top spot.

Maps

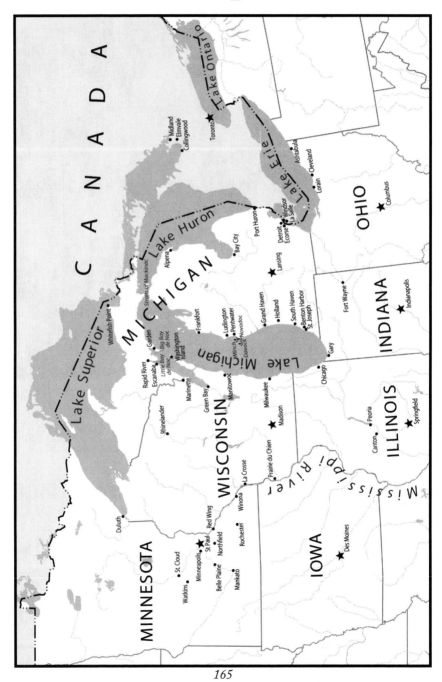

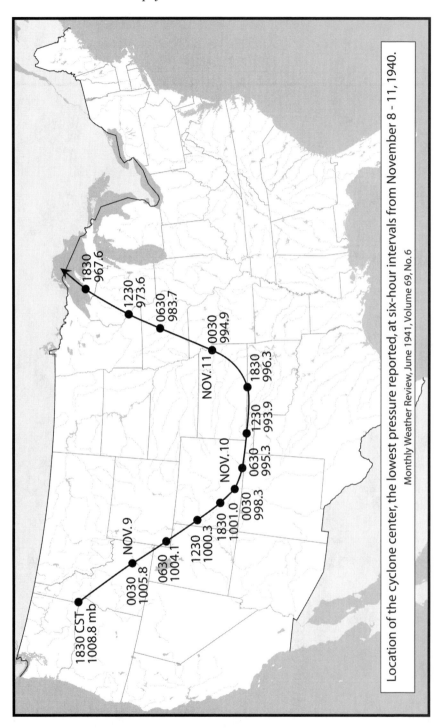

Location of the cyclone center, the lowest pressure reported, at six-hour intervals from November 8 - 11, 1940.

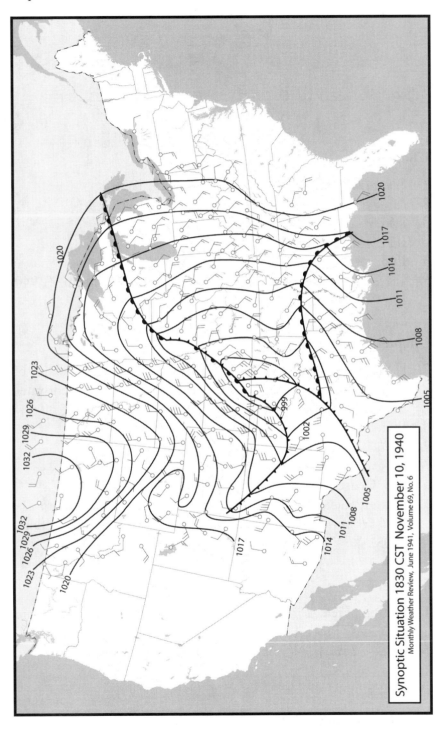

Synoptic Situation 1830 CST November 10, 1940
Monthly Weather Review, June 1941, Volume 69, No. 6

Notes

Chapter 4

1. *South Haven Daily Tribune*, November 14, 1920.
2. *Milwaukee Journal*, November 12, 1940.
3. Ibid.
4. Ibid.
5. Ibid.
6. The Carferries of the Great Lakes: Armistice Day Storm of 1940, http://www.carferries.com.

Chapter 5

7. U.S. Coast Guard, Record of Proceedings of a Board of Investigation convened at Pentwater Station, Pentwater, Michigan, November 25, 1940, p. 89.
8. Ibid.
9. *Daily Tribune* (South Haven, MI), November 13, 1940.
10. *Milwaukee Journal*, November 15, 1940.
11. U.S. Coast Guard, Record of Proceeding, p.90.
12. Mixter, Rick, *Lake Fury: Storms of the Century. Safe Ashore: The 1940 Armistice Day Storm,* (Saginaw: Airworthy Productions, 2005).

Chapter 6

13. Dutton, Fred, *Life on the Great Lakes* (Detroit: Wayne State University Press, 1991), p. 148.
14. *Chicago Tribune*, November 14, 1940.

Chapter 8

15. *Milwaukee Journal*, November 12,1940.

Chapter 9

16. Winona Republican-Herald, November 13, 1940.

Chapter 10

17. Nistler, Michael, *1st 100 Years of Watkins and St. Anthony Church,* (privately published), p. 108.
18. Ibid., p. 107.
19. Winona Republican-Herald, November 12, 1940.
20. St. Louis Park Historical Society, Minneapolis, MN, http://www.slphistory.org/history/armisticedayblizzard.asp.

Chapter 11

21. Daily Tribune, November 14,1940.
22. Ludington Daily News, November 13, 1940.
23. Daily Tribune, November 14, 1940.
24. U.S. Coast Guard, Record of Proceedings, p. 94.
25. Ibid., p.95.
26. Ludington Daily News, November 16, 1940.
27. Ibid.

Chapter 12

28. U.S. Coast Guard, Record of Proceedings, p. 71.
29. U.S. Coast Guard, Report of Assistance Serial #23, November 11, 1940.
30. U.S. Coast Guard. Letter from Chief Boatswain A.E. Kristofferson: Ludington Station to Commander, Chicago District, November 16, 1940.
31. U.S. Coast Guard, Report of Proceedings, p. 34.
32. Milwaukee Journal, November 13, 1940.
33. Belcher, Lloyd, "Sailor Recalls November 1940 Disaster," *Nor'easter,* Vol. 16, no. 5 (Sept-Oct 1991), p. 3.

Chapter 14

34. Mitchell, John G., "U.P.," *Audubon Magazine,* November 1981.

35. *Escanaba Daily Press*, November 14, 1940.
36. Ibid.

Chapter 15

37. *Winona Republican-Herald*, November 13, 1940.
38. *Milwaukee Journal*, November 13, 1940.

Chapter 16

39. *Winona Republican-Herald*, November 13, 1940.
40. Ibid.
41. Ibid.

Chapter 17

42. *Daily Tribune*, November 14, 1940.
43. *Ludington Daily News*, November 14, 1940.

Chapter 18

44. U.S. Coast Guard, Record of Proceeding, p. 91.
45. Ibid., p. 5.
46. *Ludington Daily News*, November 13, 1940.
47. Shelak, Benjamin J., *Shipwrecks of Lake Michigan*, (Black Earth, WI: Trails Books, 2003), p. 149.

Chapter 19

48. *Ludington Daily News*, November 14, 1940.
49. *Flint Journal*, November 14,1940.
50. Parsons, R. W., "The Storm of 1940," *Inland Seas*, Vol. 17, no. 3 (Fall, 1961), p. 206
51. *Milwaukee Journal*, November 14, 1940.
52. *Great Lakes News*, December 1940, p. 7

Chapter 20

53. *Winona Republican Herald*, November 19, 1940.

Chapter 21

54. Ludington Daily News, November 15, 1940.

Chapter 22

55. U.S. Coast Guard, Record of Proceedings, tp,
56. U.S. Coast Guard, Review and Recommendations by G.T. Finlay, Captain U.S.C.G. Commander, Chicago District. Chicago, Illinois, December 23, 1940 of the Record of Proceedings of a Board of Investigation convened at Pentwater Station, Pentwater, Michigan, November 25, 1940.
57. Ibid.
58. U.S. Coast Guard, Record of Proceedings, p. 96.
59. Great Lakes Journal, November 1940, p. 6.
60. Ibid.

Bibliography

Books

Bohnak, Karl. *So Cold a Sky: Upper Michigan Weather Stories.* Negaunee: Cold Sky Publishing, 2006.

Bowen, Dana Thomas. *Memories of the Lake.* Daytona Beach: D.T. Bowen, 1946.

Boyer, Dwight. *Strange Adventures of the Great Lakes.* Cleveland: Freshwater Press, Inc., 1974.

Brown, David G. *White Hurricane: A Great Lakes November Gale and America's Deadliest Maritime Disaster.* Camden: International Marine, 2002.

Buegeleisen, Sally. *Into the Wind: The Story of Max Conrad.* New York: Random House, 1973.

Dutton, Fred W. *Life on the Great Lakes: A Wheelman's Story.* Detroit: Wayne State University Press, 1991.

Hull, William H. *All Hell Broke Loose.* Edina, MN: William H. Hull, 1985.

Nistler, Michael. *The First Hundred Years of Watkins and St. Anthony Church.* Watkins: Michael Nistler, 1989.

Pyron, Darden Asbury. *Liberace: An American Boy.* Chicago: University of Chicago Press, 2000.

Shelak, Benjamin J. *Shipwrecks of Lake Michigan.* Black Earth, WI: Trails Books, 2003.

Newspapers

Bay City Times (Bay City, MI), 12–13 November 1940.

Chicago Tribune, 11–14 November 1940; 17 November 1968.

Cleveland Plain Dealer, 12–13 November 1940.

Cleveland Press, 12–13 November 1940.

Daily Mining Journal (Marquette, MI), 13 November 1940.

Daily Tribune (South Haven, MI), 12–18 November 1940.

Detroit Free Press, 11–13 November 1940.

Detroit News, 11–13 November 1940.

East County Daily Californian, 9 November 1986.

Escanaba Daily Press, 12–15 November 1940.

Flint Journal (Flint, MI), 11–14 November 1940; 1 December 2002.

Forest Lake Times (Forest Lake, MN), 8 November 1990.

Herald Journal (Minneapolis, MN), 8 November 2004.

Lorain Journal (Lorain, OH), 12 November 1940.

Ludington Daily News, 12–18 November 1940.

Milwaukee Journal, 12–15 November 1940.

Minneapolis Morning Tribune, 12–16 November 1940.

Nicollet Leader (Nicollet, MN), 15 November 1940.

Port Huron Times-Herald (Port Huron, MI), 12 November 2006.

Republican News and St. Ignace Enterprise (St, Ignace, MI), 11 November 1940.

St. Peter Herald (St. Peter, MN), 14 November 1940.

Toledo Blade, 12–13 November 1940.

Toronto Evening Telegram, 12–13 November 1940.

Vernon Center News (Vernon Center, MN), 14 November 1940.

Winona Republican-Herald (Winona, MN), 12–19 November 1940; 16 November 1940.

Periodicals

"Armistice Day Storm of 1940." *Telescope* (November–December 1995): 153–155.

"The Armistice Day Storm of 1940." *Detroit Marine Historian* 44, no. 5 (January 1991): 1–4.

"The Armistice Day Storm of 1940 – Conclusion." *Detroit Marine Historian* 44, no. 6 (February 1991): 1–4.

Belcher, Lloyd. "Sailor Recalls November 1940 Disaster." *The Nor'Easter* 16, no. 5 (September–October 1991): 1–4.

Bylander, C.B. "Death on the Mississippi." *The Minnesota Volunteer* (November–December 1990): 15–18.

Desperes, Louis R. "Treasure Ship." *Skin Diver* (November 1960): 26–27.

Knarr, Aurel J. "The Midwest Storm of November 11, 1940." *Monthly*

Weather Review 69, no. 6 (June 1941): 171–178.

Martin, R.L. "The Captain's Log: The City of Miwaukee and the Great Armistice Day Storm of 1940." *Rails Across the Water* 1, no. 1 (Fall 2000): 1+.

Mitchell, John. "U.P." *Audubon Magazine* (November 1981): 39+.

"November Gales Batter Shipping on Lake Michigan." *The Great Lakes Journal* 9, no. 10 (November 1940): 1+.

O'Meara, T. "The Big Blow." *Inland Seas* 2, no. 4 (October 1946): 236–239.

Parsons, Captain R. W. "The Storm of 1940." *Inland Seas* 17, no. 3 (Fall 1961): 202–206.

Pernick, Steve. "In the Eye of the Storm: Recollections of the Great Blizzard of 1940." *Crossing* (January 1991): 1+.

Sherin, Ray. "Cold as Death." *Outdoor Life* 116, no. 4 (October 1955): 57+.

Valentine, Sean. "Armistice Day 1940: The Storm Remembered." *The Minnesota Volunteer* (November–December 1985): 21–24.

Public Documents

Exchequer Court of Canada. *Report to the Honorable the Minister of Transport re Formal Investigation into the Circumstances Attending the floundering of the SS Anna C. Minch on or about the 12th day of November, 1940.* Toronto, Canada. February 28, 1941.

U.S. Coast Guard. *Record of Proceedings of a Board of Investigation Convened at Pentwater Station, Pentwater, Michigan.* November 25, 1940.

U.S. Coast Guard. *Record of Assistance Serial #23.* November 11, 1940. Prepared by Roland D. Ericson, Surfman Grand Haven Lifeboat Station.

U.S. Coast Guard. *Report of Assistance Serial #19.* November 11–14, 1940. Prepared by Alexander Rouleau, Ludington Lifeboat Station.

U.S. Coast Guard. *Letter from Chief Boatswain (L) A.E. Kristofferson: Ludington Station to Commander, Chicago District.* November 16, 1940.

U.S. Coast Guard. *Review and Recommendations of G.T. Finlay, Captain U.S.C.G Commander, Chicago District, Chicago, Illinois, December 23, 1940 of the Record of Proceedings of a Board of Investigation Convened at Pentwater Station, Pentwater, Michigan.* November 25, 1940.

Web sites

Armistice Day Storm of November 11, 1940 Ludington Michigan http://carferry.info/Holmes.html.

Clyde Cross — An All American Hero. http://perdurabo10.tripod.com/ships/id20.html.

The Carferries of the Great Lakes: Armistice Day Storm of 1940. http://www.carferries.com/armistice/.

St. Louis Park Historical Society. http://www.slphistory.org.

Great Lakes Shipwreck Museum. Shipwreck Stories. Survivor Recalls Sinking of the Novadoc - November 11, 1940. http://www.shipwreckmuseum.com/stories.phtml?artid=53.

Michigan Shipwreck Research Associates. Minch, Davock &

Novadoc. http://www.michiganshipwrecks.org/armistice.htm.

Michigan Shipwreck Research Associates. Richard H. http://www.michiganshipwrecks.org/richardh.htm.

DVD

Mixter, Rick. *Lake Fury: Storms of the Century. Safe Ashore: The 1940 Armistice Day Storm.* Saginaw: Airworthy Productions. 2003.

OTHER

Sturm, Monica. "The Night of the Wind: The Armistice Day Blizzard of 1940." Kitty Lieb. Historic Essay Series. New Ulm: Brown County Historical Society. 2005.

Lake Carrier's Association Annual Report. Cleveland. 1940.

About the Author

Tom Powers retired from the Flint Public Library as Head of Adult Services in 1999 after 31 years of service in order to pursue writing, reading, and laughter, to rediscover the joys of coaching youth hockey, and to continue his quest for the best piece of pie to be found in northern Michigan. He's already found the best chocolate cake. For the moment, he has put off his pursuit of a black belt in procrastination, although Barbara, his wife of 44 years, may argue that point.

Powers' first book, *Natural Michigan*, was published in 1987; the first edition of *Michigan State and National Parks: A Complete Guide* appeared in 1989. The latter book is in its fourth edition and still in print. His other books include *Michigan in Quotes, Audubon Guide to National Wildlife Refuges: Northern Midwest, Great Birding in the Great Lakes,* and *Michigan Rogues, Desperados and Cut-throats.*

Among the author's other memorable achievements was the creation of the world's first Mime Radio Show and the Julia A. Moore Poetry Festival, which honored America's worst poet. Powers steadfastly denies the Mime Radio Show was in any way responsible for the radio station's demise.

Powers deserves much less credit for the five remarkable grandchildren that continuously brighten his life.